Train of Innocents

The Story of the Kennedy Train

by
Everell Cummins

authorHOUSE™

1663 LIBERTY DRIVE, SUITE 200
BLOOMINGTON, INDIANA 47403
(800) 839-8640
WWW.AUTHORHOUSE.COM

First published by AuthorHouse 08/30/05

ISBN: 1-4208-7079-3 (e)
ISBN: 1-4208-7078-5 (sc)

Library of Congress Control Number: 2005906785

Printed in the United States of America
Bloomington, Indiana

This book is printed on acid-free paper.

Acknowledgements

Most of the source material on which this book is based came from the collections of others, who, when they learned I was interested in the Kennedy train, freely sent me copies of material they had unearthed. I would particularly like to thank the following good people (alphabetically listed):

Elaine Koll Andersen, of Sun City, AZ furnished me with a copy of a photo of John Knox Kennedy and his wife, Sarah. She also supplied information about her ancestor, Robert Kennedy, cousin of John Kennedy, with whom John spent a winter in Waitsburg, Washington Territory, a visit that seems to have prompted John Kennedy to organize the trip west.

Lee Christenson of Annapolis, MD, started me on the Kennedy train by calling my attention to the Kennedy train roster, prepared by Pat Packard and Marjorie Ellis Miles.

Bill Collier, now deceased, helped with research and computer smarts.

Roger Duba, of San Rafael, CA provided research and expertise on the Oregon Trail.

Richard Engeman, Director of Manuscripts and Archives Collection and others of the Oregon

Historical Society provided copies of the two versions of the James. S. McClung journals and explanatory background information about those documents.

My sister, Helen Cummins Holden of Los Altos, CA, provided copies of source material she had saved over the years, including an early copy of the Jane Gould diary.

Fred Howey of San Rafael, CA helped every time my computer didn't understand what I wanted it to do.

My cousin, Zola Burnap Irwin, now deceased, sent me mountains of Cummins family genealogical research over the years, as well as copies of several newspaper interviews she had kept in her collection. Some of her collection dated back to material collected by her mother, Hettie Cummins Barnes, my father's sister.

Marcine Ellis Lehman, of Beaverton, OR, descendant of Susan Frances Ellis Zaring, sent me copies of a number of documents from her collection; also she visited the Oregon Historical Society Library and provided an eye witness account of the McClung journal material in their files.

Ella Jane Allison McCarley of Battleground, WA, great, great granddaughter of John Knox Kennedy, provided all the information about the ancestry and personal history of Kennedy himself from her manuscript, "John Knox Kennedy, Pioneer of Washington State"; she also provided updated information about the Kennedy train roster and copies of newspaper interviews and other source material.

Marjorie Ellis Miles and Pat Packard of Nampa, ID, descendants of Kennedy train pioneers and authors of the Kennedy train roster, provided much encouragement as well as copies of material in their files.

My cousin Mildred Hanson Pentecost of Walla Walla, WA, undertook a field trip to Waitsburg at my request, there locating the graves of John K. and Sarah Kennedy and information about residence in Waitsburg and Dayton.

The Smith Ranch Writers Group, of San Rafael, CA, read and critiqued many portions of the book, before it became a book.

Table of Contents

Why Did They Go?

On the 24th of April, 1862, a little group of people brought together by John Knox Kennedy, left Fremont, Iowa, heading west for Walla Walla and other destinations in Eastern Washington and Oregon. Most of the earlier trains over the Oregon Trail had gone on to the Willamette Valley, but by 1862 with a US Army cavalry detachment now stationed in Walla Walla to provide protection against possible Indian attack, Walla Walla had become an attractive destination for overland travelers.

The attraction was the vast and largely untouched fertile farmland stretching across much of Eastern Washington and Oregon. By 1862 the small village of Walla Walla was primarily a supply point for the mining industry of Northern Idaho and Montana. Kennedy's train was one of the first to bring farmers to Walla Walla, people intent on doing something with that fertile soil. It was an important event in the history of the Pacific Northwest. The nucleus of Kennedy's train were farmers from Mahaska and Wapello Counties Iowa, who had sold their Iowa farms anticipating settling on farmland in the Walla Walla Valley, at a time when farming in that area was still in its infancy.

After a particularly difficult crossing, a number of these Iowa farmers reached Walla Walla and settled on the newly opened farmlands there. We know who many of the members of the Kennedy train were. We know when they left and the events that occurred during the crossing. We know where many of them settled.

Much of that kind of information we know from diaries kept by two members of the Kennedy train, some later memoirs and newspaper stories written about some of these pioneers decades later. What we don't know and what we can't know for sure about most of them is why. Why did these heads of families sell their farms and possessions in Iowa to raise the funds necessary to purchase the overland wagons, oxen to pull the wagons, provisions for the trip and the cash stake needed to get established at their destinations? While land in frontier Eastern Washington could be acquired for much less than the going price in Iowa, the cost of the trip and resettlement was substantial and the risks formidable.

Moreover, the money necessary to outfit a family for such a trip and finance subsistence and resettlement was enough to indicate these people weren't doing badly where they were. They had fertile Iowa farms, houses and livestock. While young single men James McClung and Hamilton Scott, who kept diaries of their trip, had no families to support and didn't need as large a stake as the family men, they too needed some funds, perhaps provided by whatever wages they earned on the trip hired out to heads of families who needed their help to drive and care for their livestock.

Because he told us in his diary, we do know why James McClung joined the wagon train heading west. He told us in the first page of his diary:

"I being a farmer's son after many years of hard labor, I had arrived to the age of 21...being very hard as it is in times of war and I having always had a great anxiety to cross the plains, concluded that I would seek my fortune elsewhere. I wanted to see the snow capped mountains and chase the antelope and the black tailed deer and see the grizzly bear so...I started for the gold diggings on the Salmon River." (For readability, some spelling and punctuation changes have been made in McClung's narrative.)

McClung's explanation of why he decided to "seek his fortune elsewhere" gives a variety of reasons why he left Iowa: the hard times caused by the Civil War, then a year old; the hard work on the farm; the lure of gold mining riches, and the chance to see the strange sights of the West, grizzly bears, antelope and snow capped mountains. Reading between the lines, McClung seems to have been bored stiff and ready for adventure, some adventure other than service as a Union Army soldier. While in the spring of 1862 there was still no military conscription, young men his age were volunteering for military service in droves. McClung had other plans for adventure which he found in full measure on the Kennedy train, even though he never got close to the Salmon River gold mines he mentioned as his destination.

We also know why 16 year old Margaret Stoot went along. She had no choice. John K. Kennedy, Captain of the train was her step-father. In a 1926 Walla Walla newspaper article we learn that young Margaret did not want to go west and why:

"I didn't want to leave Iowa, for my sweetheart had enlisted in an Iowa regiment and I was afraid if we made the long trip across the plains to Oregon, something would happen and we'd never get married. I was only 16 and had no folks to stay with so when my step-father and mother and the rest of the family got ready for the trip across the plains in the spring of 1862, about the only thing I could do was go along. With soldiers moving around as they did during the Civil War and with letters getting lost, my lover didn't get my letter, and of course, when we left we didn't know where we were going to settle, so he didn't know where to write to me."

As it turned out, Margaret's concern about losing contact with her sweetheart was well-founded and there was no happily ever after in her story. However, the most surprising thing about Margaret Stoot's sad tale, told 64 years later is her statement that her step-father, the leader of the wagon train "didn't know where we were going to settle."

If John K. Kennedy didn't have a specific destination planned, perhaps nobody did. Kennedy, the leader of the train was the only member of the party to have crossed the plains before. He had spent a winter with his cousin Robert P. Kennedy near Waitsburg in Walla Walla County two years before and when he returned to Iowa, he talked up the trip and the rich farmland waiting for settlement in the Walla Walla area to his neighbors. With his brother-in-law John G. McGuire, he organized the Wapello County/Mahaska County wagon train. Still, he seems to have had no specific destination or property in mind and, in fact settled his own family initially in Eastern Oregon near La Grande, rather than Walla Walla.

It's hard to comprehend how people like Kennedy and the others with him, particularly the ones with small children, such as my great-grandfather Robert Cummins, could have found the self assurance to set off into the unknown with their large families. Both the Kennedy and Cummins families included five children. It seems to us today they were on a trapeze without a net. Yet, my ancestor Robert Cummins sold his property in Iowa and joined the Kennedy train, taking along his wife and five small children, without having a definite destination or plan and knowing no one in the Walla Walla area.

In 1901 Robert Cummins wrote a brief account of his trip over the Oregon Trail with the Kennedy train, a narrative that, like most of the accounts of others was silent as to why he decided to take his family of five children, ages six months to nine years, on a difficult five month trip 1500 miles west.

Writing about his arrival in Walla Walla in September 1862, Cummins noted "Barry Gholson was the first man I met after coming west that I knew. After looking around for some time, I bought a claim located seven miles south and east of Walla Walla..." While he seems to have run into an old neighbor accidentally after arriving in Walla Walla, it is clear Cummins was not met by a welcoming party of relatives or friends on arrival. It also tells us he did not know where he would settle until he looked around "for some time". His experience was probably typical.

Restlessness and the impetus to move west seems to have been programmed into him. The trip west with Kennedy was not Cummins' first resettlement trip. At the age of one in 1831 Cummins was part of a family migration 800 miles west from the West Virginia mountains to new lands being opened in Indiana. Twenty years later, the day before his 21st birthday, Cummins married Lucretia Myers, a girl from a neighboring farm and they moved west together to newly opened land in Mahaska County, Iowa. Eleven years later, when his neighbor John K. Kennedy talked up a trip west, Cummins needed little persuasion to take another leap into the unknown.

It's more difficult to understand the decisions made by Thomas Paul and Ellis E. Ellis, both charter member families of the dozen or so wagons that started from Wapello County. Both of their wives were six months pregnant as the wagon train left Wapello County in 1862. Surely both Elizabeth Mortimore Paul and Eliza Jane Zaring Ellis must have been pregnant when the decision was made, several months earlier to undertake the trip. What were they thinking?

We can only wonder how their decisions to undertake the journey came about. Thomas Paul was 33 years old; his wife Elizabeth, 32. They took with them six other children, ages 2,4,6,8,10 and 12. While there is no way to know, considering the customs of the time we can wonder whether Elizabeth was even consulted in the decision. Moreover, it's hard to understand how anyone, husband or wife, could have concluded it would be OK to start west on a wagon train knowing the wife would come to term three months down the road during the most difficult part of the trip.

Perhaps family ties had something to do with the decision. His cousin, Robert Cummins was making the trip; also his father Joseph Paul and his mother Mary Cummins Paul. Most of the people in the Iowa nucleus were related by blood or marriage.

Ellis E. Ellis and his pregnant wife Eliza Jane had no other children, but otherwise had the same factors to consider in making a decision as the

Pauls, whether to embark on a difficult five month wagon trip, knowing the wife would have to bear a child along the way.

Thinking now about the chances of these women surviving childbirth on the trail, what would you think their chances were? They must have fully realized the chancy nature of successfully bearing a child en-route, yet they went and there is no evidence of any agonizing over the decision to go.

You could also question the decision Thomas Paul's parents made. His father Joseph, a minister and his mother Mary were both 56 years old at the start of the trip, considered incredibly old for the time, to be taking such a trip. However, it's easier to understand why Joseph Paul decided to go. He seems to have been the unofficial minister for the wagon train and had occasion to preach many sermons along the way to the members of the wagon train. He was pursuing his calling, saving souls, but was also charged with the responsibility of invoking the almighty to protect the train through the perils of the trip, an effort, as it turned out, not notably successful.

A Pleasurable Trip

Seventy years later, Sarah Zaring Howard wrote about the genesis of the Kennedy train: "The Captain had pictured to his people a pleasurable trip with camping, fishing, hunting and traveling at leisure. However things were not always what they seemed and each day brought new trials. It seemed that we were somewhat like the children of Israel when they were wandering in the desert, and some felt like faltering by the wayside but they did not turn back."

That first month on the trail may have been pleasant, assuming the travelers could enjoy whole families living together in a small box on a covered wagon and at least they were on their way and traveling through settled country and were able to buy food and supplies in the towns along the way. Reading what James McClung and Hamilton Scott wrote, the first month of the Kennedy wagon train's trip west may have been the "pleasurable trip with...traveling at leisure" Kennedy had advertised. It was certainly leisurely. The train covered only about 230 miles that first month.

From Scott's first entry: "I started April 24 in company with Thomas Paul, Rev. Joseph Paul, Alvin Zaring and families from near Fremont, Iowa for Walla Walla, Washington Territory. We loaded our wagons and drove eight miles", to his entry a month later on May 24: "This is our first camp on what we might call the real plains. It is just one month today since we bid adieu to home and friends and cracked our whips for the Pacific Coast or the gold mines we hope to find beyond the Rocky Mountains", progress averaged less than half the 15-20 miles a day considered standard. Most of the slow pace was accounted for by the ten day delay along the Missouri River, laying in provisions and waiting for additional wagons.

While travel through settled, civilized country may have been pleasurable, only twice during the first month did the 26 year old Hamilton Scott note leisure activities: "practiced shooting" on April 28 and "fished but had no luck" on May 7. Mostly his diary of the first month simply notes where they were each day and such facts as the condition of the cattle.

In contrast, James McClung's diary entrees are often lengthy descriptions of the countryside and the events he observes, but he is silent on any leisure activities. Perhaps keeping his diary was the important leisure activity for young McClung. As an example of his entries during the first month, on May 1 he wrote: "The roads slippery, the weather cool, in about 3 miles we came to a creek called Cedar, after which we passed through low scrubby timber and brush on to the prairie which was very broken...camped near a farmer's house who furnished us corn at 20 cents a bushel [and] hay 25 cents per hundred."

On May 23 he wrote that "a little boy belonging to Mr. McCormick fell out of the wagon, the wheel running over his foot, breaking some of the bones." McClung misses very little and tries to give us, his latter day readers, a complete account of what he saw and experienced. While McClung used expressive language in his diary, the original spelling was largely phonetic and the punctuation absent.

Scott reported the same accident, though he failed to mention the boy's name: "One of the small boys got his leg broken by falling out of the wagon he was riding and the wheel passed over his leg." While both McClung and Scott were young single men and both original members of the group, neither ever mentions the other in his diary and it is apparent they did not compare notes and were not in close contact. Often, as in this case, a discrepancy between the accounts remains unresolved. Was it a leg or a foot?

By 1862 the overland trail west was a well-traveled road. An estimated 265,000 people had passed over it. Guidebooks described every mile. The Army issued widely distributed advisories as to what was needed in the way of wagons, supplies and animal power to successfully complete the trip. One such advisory, issued by Captain Medorem Crawford in 1862, provided highly explicit advice:

- "Mules and oxen should be used for teams. Horses will not do...best teams are medium sized active young oxen."
- "Plenty of wagon grease should be provided and freely used."
- "Each person should take at least 250 pounds of provisions; one half of which should be flour, 50 pounds bacon and the balance in sugar, coffee, tea, rice, dried fruits etc."
- "Each man should be well armed."
- "Your captain should decide and order when to start, when and where to camp and his orders should be implicitly obeyed. He should decide all disputes and his decisions should be final whether right or wrong."
- "For guard duty, the men should be equally divided into three divisions or squads, one of which is constantly on duty."
- "Take no dogs along." (The Kennedy train ignored that advice, which caused serious dissension later in the trip.)

Reading Hamilton Scott's diary entry of May 24 now, generations later, we have to sorely regret that the only known diaries of the trip were kept by two young single men. Scott recorded the following in his diary: "...camped at noon to allow the women to do some washing. We boys went swimming." We can only wonder what those women would have written had they kept diaries.

Perhaps, busy washing the clothes, they could not find the time for a diary. Young James McClung failed to mention swimming, noting only: "We traveled 13 miles and camped to wash and cook." He did not record who did the washing and who did the cooking. McClung must have assumed his readers would have known that washing and cooking were women's work.

A Courthouse on Wheels

On May 22, now 35 miles west of Omaha, camped on the banks of the Platte River, James McClung reported on an important event, an organizational meeting called by Kennedy. The wagon train was now on the edge of the open plains and the end of all civil law. There would be no more judges, no more sheriffs, and no more county clerks. According to McClung, "After supper we were called together for the purpose of organizing ourselves into a company. Our constitution and bylaws having been written out and adopted, we then proceeded to the choice of officers by election. John K. Kennedy was elected Captain; John McGuire, First Lieutenant; Second Lieutenant, Thomas Paul; Third Lieutenant, J. W. Cramer; Orderly, James Standfield; Second Sergeant, J. Ornduff; R. Cummins, Justice of the Peace."

Forty-one years later, Robert Cummins wrote a confirming account of his memory of the meeting. "We organized [and] made our laws which we were to be governed by on our journey west. Officers elected were: John Kennedy, Captain; Robert Cummins, Judge; James Standfield, Corporal and Constable."

One western historian wrote about wagon train bylaws: "During the early years of overland emigration, companies frequently wrote constitutions and adopted bylaws before they started out on the trail. The practice was largely discontinued after the 1850 emigration. By then most emigrants knew that few companies would remain united and rules could be made ad hoc to deal with problems as they arose."

While it was no longer a common practice by 1862, Kennedy reverted to the earlier custom and made a special effort to bind his company to written rules. Moreover, designating these written rules as "laws", "bylaws", or a "constitution", as Kennedy did, converted the company into something very much like a governmental body, a kind of courthouse on wheels. The fact that the whole company heard the "laws" read and voted to approve them contributed to the sense of obligation the members felt to him and to the company as a whole and led them to see their company as a legitimate civil authority. Perhaps Kennedy also reasoned that, bound by their agreement to his authority as Captain, the members would view "his decisions as final, whether right or wrong", as Army Captain Crawford had admonished.

In the end however, the adopted constitutions and bylaws did not keep the train intact, nor did the members always view his decisions as final "whether right or wrong." Later in the trip, after some had refused guard duty, McClung characterized the company as "contrary." Bernard DeVoto in his Year of Decision: 1846 commented on the limits of the authority of wagon train leaders: "The captain's duties were large, but his authority was theoretical; everyone had the inalienable privilege of dissent and especially of criticism."

These Iowans Kennedy had brought together for the trip west were not an exception to DeVoto's comment. These self-reliant Iowa farmers were not used to taking orders from anyone. Seemingly every important decision Kennedy was to make on the trip alienated some faction in the train, as he attempted to keep control of his wagon train.

Kennedy had a practical reason for keeping tight control over his company: Indians. When the first wagon trains crossed the overland trail to Oregon and California in the early 1840s, they faced few problems with Indians, even though there were few if any Army troops along the trail. Later, as the number of emigrants increased along the route, grievances grew. Some of the tribes became more hostile and attacks on wagon trains became more common. To protect the emigrants, Army cavalry posts were set up along the route. However, the Army's relations with the Indians seem to have worsened the problem and some previously friendly tribes turned hostile to all whites, after incidents with the cavalry.

By 1862 emigrants crossing the trail to the west needed the protection offered by the Cavalry. But President Lincoln had a greater need for those same troops in the East to fight the Civil War battles then raging and that is where most of them went. Some of the veteran troops were replaced by inexperienced volunteers, such as those from Ohio who manned Fort Laramie in Eastern Wyoming, but other long stretches of the trail were entirely stripped of Army troops. The Indians sensed the weakening and stepped up their aggressions.

In the 1840s, before Indian hostility had increased, guidebooks and advisories recommended ten to fifteen wagons as the optimum range. Wagon trains traveled no faster than the slowest ox team, the recommended motive power. The more wagons in the train, the slower the progress; the slower the progress, the more provisions had to be carried. Large wagon trains also had difficulties with stampedes, so the safety supposedly offered by a large wagon train was gained at considerable cost. Army Captain Medorum Crawford's advisory recommended thirty to sixty wagons per train, indicating a minimum of thirty for safety.

Kennedy started from Wapello County Iowa with a nucleus of only a dozen of so wagons. Somehow he had made arrangements with a few others to join the party at the Missouri River crossing, but he still needed more and got them while waiting and provisioning along the Missouri, merging with other small parties waiting there. As he moved west from Omaha, Kennedy had a highly organized, well-provisioned train totaling 52 wagons, manned by 222 men, women and children.

Kennedy had selected the people going with him to the West and had seen to the proper provisioning of the train as well as to the organization of the train into a functioning disciplined entity. The members of his party, or at least the original nucleus who had been his neighbors, had reason to put their trust in Kennedy to get them to their destination safely. They were well aware of the dangers of a trip west that year, but they knew his background and experience and had reason to view him as the ideal leader for the trip.

Who Was John Knox Kennedy?

Taking the command of a wagon train company on the overland trail posed an unusual set of challenges to the management and leadership skills of anyone who attempted it. To do the job to the satisfaction of the heads of families in the company was almost impossible, even for an experienced and fully prepared leader. A look at Kennedy's background and his careful preparation for the trip confirms Kennedy as ready for the job and allows us to understand why the members of his party were willing to trust him with what they knew to be a hazardous endeavor. Moreover, we can understand better why, when trouble arose on the trail, as it did, emigrants on other wagon trains looked to Kennedy for leadership and action.

Kennedy was born in 1811 in Greene County Tennessee, second son of Samuel and Frankey Kennedy. He married Sarah Steele there in 1830 and in 1831 John, Sarah and related families moved to newly opened land in Hancock County Indiana and in 1839, continuing following the westward movement of the frontier, relocated again to newly opened land in Morgan County Illinois. By 1842 John and Sarah had five children: James, Frankey, Rhoda Ann, Robert and Mary Elizabeth. In 1845 John's wife Sarah died.

In May 1847, with the Mexican War on, widower John enlisted in the Army at Savannah, Missouri as a First Sergeant. He took his not quite 16 year old son James with him, leaving the younger children with relatives. Kennedy was assigned to a battalion of Missouri mounted volunteers commanded by Lt. Col. Ludwell E. Powell and his son was employed in a civilian capacity. Powell's battalion was given the job of establishing military posts along the overland trail to Oregon and California. Kennedy participated in establishing a post on the Platte River, a post first named Fort Childs, then later renamed Fort Kearny.

While employed in the battalion, his young son James was killed by Indians in October 1847. Could there be some connection between his son's death at the hands of Indians and Kennedy's later extreme emphasis on protecting his wagon train from hostile Indians? Shortly after his son's death Kennedy was disciplined and reduced in rank to private, but we don't know the circumstances or what if any connection there might have been to his son's death.

Neither of the surviving trip diaries notes any hostility or cruelty to Indians on Kennedy's part and his preparations for Indian hostilities seem appropriate for the time. Still, the research of one of Kennedy's descendants identified one member of the party who claimed to have left the Kennedy train because of Kennedy's alleged hostility to Indians. However, Kennedy's view of Indians was probably no different than most of the members of his party. Indeed, after completing the trip James McClung wrote his mother in Iowa to tell his friends to "stay there until the Indians is all killed and their wigwams scattered..."

Kennedy received an honorable discharge at Fort Leavenworth, Kansas in November 1848. As a result of his army service, Kennedy earned the right to bounty land, again on the westward moving frontier in Wapello County, Iowa, southeast of Des Moines. There he met and married a widow, Sarah Stoots, mother of three daughters and a son. They were married in 1849 and a son, John H. C. Kennedy was born the following year.

During the 1849 California gold rush, Kennedy and two neighbors traveled on the overland trail to California and on his return he sold his property in Wapello County and bought property in adjacent Mahaska County. During his years in Mahaska County, we know he was a member of the Masonic Lodge. He was county sheriff for two years and he served as a captain in the Iowa state militia. The 1860 census showed the value of his real property as $4200, indicating a sizeable farm acreage and financial solvency.

In 1859, again on the lookout for land on the frontier, Kennedy went exploring to the west, this time to Walla Walla County, Washington Territory where he spent the winter with his cousin, Robert P. Kennedy, who had settled on property on or near the site of the present day town of Waitsburg. At the time, the town of Walla Walla, close to the protection of a military detachment at Fort Walla Walla was primarily a re-supply center for the mines in Idaho and Montana. Empty, fertile land awaited settlement. On his return in the spring of 1860, Kennedy had decided to move west himself.

It seems clear that Kennedy was a respected and persuasive leader among his neighbors in Wapello and Mahaska Counties and eminently well qualified to lead a group west. His background in the military and in law enforcement, as well as his experience handling livestock and his familiarity with the trail west all helped persuade his neighbors to go with him. There may have been two other factors. Kennedy was a Mason. So was Robert Cummins. Were most of the nucleus Masons? From an incident at Independence Rock later in the trip it appears that they may have been.

Also, in a 1926 interview, one of Kennedy's stepdaughters, Margaret Stoots Thiel (who left her sweetheart to go on the trip) alleged that Kennedy had outfitted nine neighbor families with wagons and oxen so they could make the trip. They promised to pay but "he never got a cent from them."

Indians, Prairie Dogs and Buffalo Chips

Many of the sights these travelers saw along the route were totally new to them. Perhaps they had seen Indians before but certainly not in lands the Indians claimed as their own. Most of people in the train were farmers and many may not have traveled more than a few miles from their Iowa farms. McClung reported on the first Indians on May 25. "We struck Platte River in the forenoon where we saw some Indians who was living in their winter houses, yet the first we have seen....and camped near a small lake where several Indians came to see us. Our Captain gave each a small piece of tobacco and told them to 'puchahee' which they did reluctantly." One source speculates that puchachee means to leave.

Here Captain Kennedy was following the advice of the experts. Captain Medorem Crawford's advisory cautioned: "As friendly Indians often visit emigrant camps for trade, care should be taken not to be allowed inside the camp. If you have business with them, transact it outside." Another source states it is the custom "when emigrants passed through Indian Country, to give presents, powder, lead, etc."

Traveling up the Platte River McClung reports "... a severe wind and rain storm ensued that night during which our cattle broke away from the guard. [On the] 27th, we rose early, gathered up our cattle drove down to Loupe Fork where there were about 150 teams waiting to cross on one small ferry. Our train got across against sundown. We swam our cattle. Some of the cattle swum back over the river, which caused us a heap of trouble and gave us a late start."

This was the first of many problems the party had keeping track of their cattle. One authority on wagon trains noted that an "all night watch is needed, Indians or not. The guards switch on a rotation basis...every three hours."

Hamilton Scott also reported on the cattle breaking away that night. His diary for May 27 and 28 recorded: "Had quite a storm last night, cattle broke away from the guards, found them this morning not very far away. We ferried the river. There being about sixty teams ahead of us, it took all day to get across. Some of our cattle swam the river last night. We had quite a hunt for them but finally found them and made a twenty mile drive today." While most of these Iowa farmers must have known how to handle yoked oxen on their farms, they seem to have had great difficulty controlling them out on the trail, probably a much more difficult job.

Scott saw 60 teams ahead of them at the ferry; McClung saw 150. It's safe to say neither counted the teams nor read the other's diary.

By McClung's May 29th entry, the train began to experience the absence of firewood. "There is no timber except on islands which was mostly brush. There are a few settlers along here. Some live in sod houses, some live in log houses covered with sod. We traveled 21 miles on this flat, muddy bottom, camped on the river side."

On the 31st McClung records "Mr. W. H. Coons and I took our guns, and went to hunt game. We left the road about five miles. Here we saw some antelope and a jack rabbit, which was the first game of any size that we have seen. After rambling for several hours we returned to the train very much fatigued, having killed nothing of much importance." Many reports note finding little or no game near the overland trail. Thousands of hungry hunters had pretty much cleared the area of anything edible.

On the same day McClung tells us that "Near here we passed four graves; the deceased was Mr. John T. Smith and two sons and a hired hand who was killed by the Sioux Indians on February 22nd 1862 while chopping in the timber some four miles from home." As a good reporter of what he saw on the trail, McClung appears to have recorded in his diary every grave marker he noticed during the trip, far too many to include all of them here.

Two days later he writes again about antelope. "We saw several antelope but I have learned long ago it did not pay for me to hunt them." Two days later he tells us all about prairie dogs. "We frequently pass a town of prairie dogs. They live and burrow in the ground. I often noticed when passing they would come to the mouth of their den and bark at us. In shooting one of them and don't immediately get it, their fellows drag it back in their dens. Those little dogs resemble a fist pup in appearance and are about the size of a groundhog and are of a yellowish cast."

On June 6, now in Western Nebraska near the present day town of Cozad, Hamilton Scott noted two graves by the side of the trail. On one "there was a large flag waving over and the man's name inscribed on the head board. He had shot himself accidentally ten days ago and lived several hours." McClung gives us more detail. He was "Jacob Gramberling, who was shot accidentally while riding in his wagon by the discharge of his gun that was swimming in the wagon box...on May the 26th 1862...He lived seven hours afterwards. Age unknown."

Hamilton Scott's entry of June 7, 1862 testifies to the shortage of firewood. "(We) swam to an island to get wood. We got some dead willows. We are told that we get no more wood for 200 miles." McClung reported the same activity, again in more detail. "Our wood was willow brush, that was on an island in the river, which we had to swim and crop our brush by tying it in bunches and pulling it over a rope that was again pulled back by men on the island. After we got our wood, I went hunting and killed a jack rabbit." The following day he noted: "Wood is out of the question. We burn buffalo chips which is a good substitute. Here we had a prayer meeting, the first meeting we have had since we left Fremont."

Overland Trail expert Merrill Mattes writes about the need for firewood. "Wood was necessary to dry clothes, fend off the chill, cook a hot supper. Means of obtaining wood on the Prairie were: wading or swimming the river to get green willows, and stunted cottonwoods. Also, driftwood from the flood in 1861, or abandoned wagon beds, dry prairie grass, or buffalo manure, more commonly known as buffalo chips, were other ways. It took 3 to 4 bushels of buffalo chips to heat a good meal. As more emigrants went across the prairie, the harder it was to find them."

The Bravery Test

Scott and McClung continue to chronicle the day to day events of the Kennedy train, each in his own style. McClung apologized for the lack of things to report on June 12. "This being my birthday, I was 21 and being sick, I was confined to my bed pretty much all day....and of course I cannot give but a very few items in regard to this day's travels; only the wagon was continually running over rocks, into ditches almost upsetting the wagon at times, which gave me very good exercise by the way." McClung's entry for June 13 tells us he was "confined to bed half the day." No doubt the "bed" was the wagon box.

If we think of mad cow disease as a recent development, Scott's entry of June 13 puzzles. "Mr. Delong shot one of his cows this morning. She acted as if she was mad or had inflammation of the brain. Drove twenty miles today and camped on the Platte River."

On June 15, Scott tells about another stampede, the second of many. "Had an exhortation from Father Paul at nine o'clock AM. Started at half past eleven moved along very nicely until about four o'clock, when two of the boys laid down by the roadside and raised up suddenly just as a team of five yoke of cattle were passing. The team took fright and ran off to one side and turned over the wagon in a ditch, killing one ox and hurting one child, but not dangerously. The chain broke, letting four yoke loose from the wagon. We drove one mile farther and camped, making about an eight mile drive today. After we settled in the camp we decided that we could have fresh beef steak for supper. So a few of us went back and skinned the ox that was killed in the wreck and brought the hind quarters into camp. We sure had beef steak for supper and breakfast."

McClung also reported on the events of Sunday, June 15. "We stayed in camp till eleven o'clock. Mr. Paul gave us a short sermon and held a short prayer meeting. About four o'clock PM, a severe accident happened. Three or four teams got scared and started to run, upsetting a wagon, killing an ox, breaking the wagon some and hurting a child, but not dangerously." Both McClung and Scott used the same phrase, "but not dangerously." While that might indicate some communication between the two, it's interesting that McClung doesn't seem to have been a party to the butchering of the ox, nor to the feast on beefsteak.

On June 16 Hamilton Scott noted passing by Chimney Rock, a well-known landmark on the overland trail Southeast of Scott's Bluff, Nebraska. "This rock stands on a sand bar and is thirty feet high and about six feet in diameter at the top. Saw some Indians today the first for about three hundred miles. Drove twenty miles today."

On June 17, Scott reported "Tim Bailey's wife brought a newcomer into camp last night which caused us to lay by today." Other sources indicate that the Tim Bailey family was not part of the original nucleus, but members of the four wagon "Raley party" from Nebraska City, Nebraska, which joined the Kennedy train somewhere after the Missouri River crossing at Omaha. While apparently all went well, that means Mrs. Bailey gave birth less than a month after beginning a cross continent wagon train trip. Incredible!

McClung failed to note the birth of Mrs. Bailey's baby, but did note that "We remained in camp today. The women put in the day cooking and washing. Upwards of 100 teams passed us today." McClung went hunting but "killed nothing. I returned to camp very sick where Dr. D. Y. Collins was called in to see me and in a few days I was able to take my position again by the side of my team." Considering the state of medical science at the time, we can wonder what medicine Dr. Collins could have had with him to help James McClung back to health.

On June 18 the party passed Scott's Bluff, Nebraska and camped that evening on or near what is now the state line between Nebraska and Wyoming. On June 19 Scott's diary recorded "Pleasant today, drove 25 miles today and camped on the river near timber, the first for about 200 miles. We have been using weeds and buffalo chips for fuel which answered very well on these desert plains."

McClung's June 19 entry tells us more about that day. "We passed by two Indian villages. I visited them in company with some young ladies. In passing the door of one of the huts, the old chief came out and seeing a beautiful intelligent girl by the name of Miss Kennedy, he was determined on having her. But she claimed she was mine and could not stay. He then tried in every position to trade me ponies and other property for her, but it was not a good day for trading and he did not succeed." The "beautiful and intelligent girl" was undoubtedly the daughter of Captain Kennedy, probably twenty year old Mary Elizabeth. Reading between the lines you could conclude McClung had a romantic interest in Miss Kennedy. His next entry, fresh from the outing with Miss Kennedy, reports on a wedding that same evening and signals his own interest and favorable view of marriage.

"At eight o'clock PM, a couple named Mr. Chester Snider and Miss E. Fickard, from another train, after being acquainted two weeks, remembered it was said it was well not to be alone, so they came to our train and the Reverend Mr. Paul said the ceremonies in the presence of a large appreciating audience. So you see, people can marry on the plains as well as at home." Since there were no county clerks or any civil government at all in what is now Wyoming, we can wonder about the legal basis for the Snyder-Fickard union, but at the time, marriage by a minister was all that was required for a legal marriage.

Later that evening both diarists reported some excitement. McClung wrote "At eleven o'clock, we was aroused by shooting and hollering of the guards in one moment of time. The corral was filled with women and children, some crying, some praying and some scared too bad to speak. What caused the excitement, one or two Indians was seen trying to steal a horse and was fired on some 30 times or more by our guards and then escaped unhurt...We raised pretty well early and found ourselves still alive and still able to travel."

Scott tells it a little differently. "We had an alarm in camp about eleven o'clock last night. The guards called three times, 'who comes there'. This was followed by about twenty shots in quick succession, at the same time 'Indians, Indians, Indians, help, help, help!' was shouted. The camp was in great confusion, women were greatly alarmed. It turned out to be a white man trying to steal a horse and no Indians to be found."

Both wrote their diary entries the next morning and they reported the outcome two ways; McClung said it was "one or two Indians", Scott a "white man". Both were wrong. Sometime in the 1920s, Alvin Zaring, who was traveling in the same party as Scott, recalled the true story in a newspaper interview. "Captain Kennedy thought best as we were getting out among the Indians, to test the bravery of the men in the train. He fell upon the plan to have the guards raise an alarm that the Indians were coming and attacking the horse guards. This caused quite an excitement. One old fellow jumped out of his wagon and getting on his knees, called upon the Lord for protection at the very top of his voice. Judging from the old fellow's daily life, I would think it was probably the first time he had ever prayed."

Neither McClung nor Scott ever mentioned the incident again in their diaries, and we are left to wonder whether they ever knew the truth, that Kennedy had staged a fake attack, a fire drill of sorts, to see how the party would react to a real attack. From both diary accounts, it seems members of the party didn't react very well. While Scott and McClung never corrected their initial accounts, eventually all the members of Kennedy's train would have learned the truth about the "attack", that Kennedy had told them a false story about the event, a fact which could have eroded confidence in Kennedy's leadership. In a letter to his mother after the trip, McClung spoke negatively about Kennedy, including the charge that he had lied. Perhaps the "attack" story was in McClung's mind.

It would have been enlightening to have had Kennedy's version of the "bravery test", but we can only conjecture about his view of the event.

On Top of the Rock

Sunday, June 22 found the Kennedy train camped across the Platte River from Fort Laramie, about 30 miles inside what is now Wyoming. Mail waited there for some. McClung wrote: "We remained in camp while our captain, John, K. Kennedy took the list of names and went over to the post offices. The company devoted the principal part of the day in writing letters to friends we left behind us...At 3:00 o'clock PM the mail came and, as every one was anxious, of course to get a letter, they was all on hand and awaiting here. We heard from the old stomping ground for the first time, which placed anew the recollection of all that was near and dear which we left behind. Words could not describe my feelings as I read the lines of my mother's handwriting, which could not help bringing a dreary lonesome feeling over me as my mind was carried back to the early years of childhood."

In contrast to McClung's emotional reaction to his letter from home, Hamilton Scott's reaction is more reserved. Arriving near Fort Laramie on June 21, he describes the location. "The river forks here and the Fort stands in the fork of the river. Here we ate dinner and watered our cattle. There being no grass, we drove three miles up the north fork and struck camp. The women did some washing here." Then the following day, "Captain

Kennedy went over to the post office which was on the opposite side of the river. He got a great many letters but none for me which disappointed me very much. We remained in camp all day."

Starting out again on June 23, the train was now 190 miles from Independence Rock, so named because it was the location overland wagon trains were expected to reach by July the 4th. The wisdom of the day maintained that a train arriving at Independence Rock after July 4th might not make it over the last mountains before the dreaded first snowfall. For the California-bound trains, the feared early snowfalls were at Donner Pass, in the Sierra Nevada Mountains; for the Oregon emigrants the danger might appear in the Blue Mountains of Eastern Oregon. They had twelve days to make it, and from the diary entries of both young diarists, the trail over those 190 miles was very unfriendly.

Scott tells us little about those days. His entries were terse, but peppered with the language of trouble. "...about as strange and stony road as I ever traveled" (June 23). "...grass not very good" (June 24). "...grass not very good" (June 25). "...grass no good" (June 26). "Bad roads in forenoon..." (June 27). "Grass very poor (June 29). "...sagebrush for fuel" (July 2). "(Have) no grass and scarcely any water for our stock..." (July 3). Lack of grass and water for the stock was a serious problem. Those sturdy oxen pulling those heavy wagons up and down the hills mile after mile would only survive, doing their jobs with the fuel found in the grass they found along the way. Not only was the dry area they were traversing in Eastern Wyoming short of grass, the Kennedy train was competing with many other trains and the stock competing with thousands of other oxen pulling the wagons in those other trains, for the little grass that was there. Still, on July 3rd they were only 14 miles away from Independence Rock.

During those same days, McClung found much to write about and, while confirming all the difficulties Scott reported so tersely, he found beauty in the area and things that interested him to write about. On June 23rd, after noting the road as "very steep and rocky", he wrote "It is a beautiful scene, to peek over those bluffs, which is interspersed over with beautiful pine and see the stone walls which nature planted there which resembles the hand of art. In traveling 14 miles without water, we passed a beautiful spring on the right...furnishing water enough only for drinking purposes....In traveling a short distance from here, we camped on Black Water which is a dirty muddy stream nigh another spring where we got water for cooking purposes. Grass poor."

On the same day McClung reported on a trail-side grave marker. "Near here on the bluff, we passed the grave of Elvan Ingram, who died June 23rd, 1852, age 4 years, 6 months, from Salem, Iowa. It is just 10 years today since the death of this child."

There were scores of grave markers alongside the trail and McClung recorded them all in his diary.

James McClung was not in Iowa anymore and was finally seeing some of the spectacular mountain peaks he had recorded as one of the reasons for making the trip. On June 25th he noted "Traveling 15 miles without water, we camped on Cottonwood Creek." On the 26th he again commented on the scenery. "...the road leading over the bluffs opposite Laramie Peak, which we've been in sight of for a week and it's covered with snow."

McClung's entry for Sunday, June 29 vividly describes what must have been a miserable day. "...We traveled until the middle of the afternoon without water...At this time we came to a river and there was a tremendous rain come up from the west, facing us, mixed with hail. The drivers not having time to unhook their teams, they turned around in spite of their upsetting some of the wagons...But some of us got pretty tolerable wet and the afternoon was rather cool and as there was no suitable place to camp, we had to drive till late and then gather wet weeds and green willow brush to make a fire to dry and warm ourselves by. And this we got by wading the river to an island and gathering in the dark."

On July first "...we met a train of 54 Mormon wagons, going to the states to move out their brethren and sisters. They told us very (frightening?) reports about the Indians which we did not believe, but afterwards learned was so." While McClung's comment is not clear, "going to the states" probably refers to a train returning east to transport European immigrants, their "brethren and sisters", back to Utah.

On July 2 McClung writes "...left Platte River taking a drink and biding her farewell. From where we struck the Platte the 23rd of May to here it is 548 miles. The river where we first struck it was one mile wide and very shallow but the further up we came, the narrower she got and here it is not more than 50 yards wide but deep and swift." On July 3rd, now only 14 miles from Independence Rock, McClung told of "an old stage station that was taken by Indians, the horses stolen and the whites killed. At one o'clock we moved on, crossed a beautiful spring creek and camped."

Both of the diaries reported a tragedy on July 4. McClung wrote about it this way. "A day which is to be long remembered. Some of the company went out hunting. When about 4 miles from the train a man from Jefferson County (a county in Iowa east of Wapello and Mahaska counties where the train originated) by the name of George Bovee killed a wolf and in stooping over to cut off its ears, a revolver fell from his belt, the hammer striking a rock, discharged the pistol, the bullet passing through his heart, killed him instantly. The deceased left a wife and 3 small children to mourn his loss. We traveled seven miles and camped on Sweetwater, close to Independence Rock and buried the dead. This rock is quite a curiosity. It covers two acres of ground and is 100 feet high. During the day 200 (wagons) came up and camped here. About half a mile from here there was a company of soldiers stationed."

Scott wrote "...The wolf fell down a crevice between two rocks. When Bovee stooped to scalp the animal, his revolver fell from the holster, hitting a rock and shooting him through the heart. He lived only a few minutes. He leaves a wife and two children. Poor woman, it will be hard for her....The train moved on a couple of miles to Independence Rock on Sweet Water. Here we struck camp. This rock is one-fourth of a mile long, two hundred feet high and three or four hundred feet wide at the bottom and is rounding from the ground up. It has several ponds of water on top." Again, the two young diarists don't quite agree on their facts, but at least prove that they were not writing their diaries together.

McClung's prediction that the day of Bovee's death "will be long remembered" proved true. In 1932, 60 years after the event, Sarah Zaring Howard reported her memory of Bovee's death to the Garfield, Washington Women's Club."...some of the men went hunting. They had not been out very long until one man came to camp with the report that one of their number, a man who had a wife and two children in the camp, had accidentally killed himself by letting his revolver fall from his belt. His little boy, five or six years old, on hearing that his father was dead, clapped his hands and said, 'Oh, good! I'll have father's knife.' I never forgot how that boy looked. I can see him yet."

Bovee's death seems to have had a marked impact on the memories of those who survived and unloaded their recollections decades later. Late in her life, Ellen Paul Garlington, age ten in 1862, included an account of Bovee's death in her undated comments. "We camped (at Independence Rock) while some of the men hunted. One of them returned and said he had killed a wolf. The others joked him and refused to believe him, so he said he would bring in the pelt, but in stooping over, his revolver dropped and struck a rock, killing him. He was buried there."

We could ask how an experienced frontiersman could have committed such a blunder, allowing his pistol to fall from his holster. We know little about George Bovee, but do know that most of these west-bound travelers were not at all experienced in the arts of survival on the frontier. They were mostly hard-working farmers living a settled life, accustomed to at least the simple creature comforts of the time, who had joined the western migration. They tried hard to prepare and equip themselves with the firearms and the other necessities urged on them for the trip, but most of them were greenhorns, a wagon train of innocents, skilled in farming, but not really prepared for life on the overland trail.

The legend on the Wyoming Department of Highways map at Independence Rock shows "Site of the first meeting of the Masonic lodge in Wyoming, July 4, 1862". That was the date the Kennedy train arrived at Independence Rock and, according to McClung, the date 200 other western-bound wagons arrived. A Wyoming web-site covering the history of Independence Rock states "On July 4, 1862, a wagon train headed for Washington and Oregon encamped on this spot. Out of this wagon train approximately 20 Masons, who could mutually vouch for each other, traversed to the top of the Rock to hold the first tiled Masonic Communication in what is now Wyoming..."

The Kennedy train was headed to Washington and Oregon. Kennedy was a Mason. Among the more than eighty heads of families in the train, probably many more were Masons. Were Kennedy and some of the others in his train some or all of the 20 Masons who attended the meeting on top of the Rock? We don't know, but it seems a good guess that some of them were involved in the meeting.

At least we can conjecture that Hamilton Scott may have climbed to the top of the rock, since he reported there were ponds on top. His diary for July 5th told: "We laid in camp until one o'clock on account of Thomas Paul's wife being sick. She was better at noon so we hitched up. We have about eighty wagons in the train now. About five miles up the river we crossed, swimming our stock and pulling our wagons over a shaky bridge by hand...camped near Devil's Gate which the river runs through. Traveled eight miles today."

Somewhere along the way, Kennedy had recruited about thirty more wagons for his train. A month earlier the wagon count was 52. Perhaps the safety of a large, well-armed train had attracted others to join. Now, Kennedy's train was larger than the optimum 30 to 60 advocated by Captain Crawford in his advisory.

In McClung's July 5th entry he makes no mention of the illness of the pregnant Elizabeth Paul, but does record an important event ignored by Scott. "Remained in camp till noon. Here we again learned that the Indians was still robbing and committing awful depredations among the emigrants. So we formed ourselves into a military company called the Independent Braves, to go in advance of the team so as to be ready at any time we needed it."

When Kennedy crossed the Missouri at Omaha, leaving all civil law behind, he organized his wagon train to take the place of the sheriffs and judges and written laws east of the Missouri. Now, nearing the end of Army protection, he had decided to supplant the protection they had enjoyed from the presence of soldiers along the trail by creating his own mounted militia. The last mention in either diary of U.S. Army soldiers along the route was just five days later. After that it certainly appears there were no soldiers at all along the trail until the train reached what is now Western Idaho. The Independent Braves were not the U.S Cavalry – too green for that – but they were the closest thing to the cavalry on that part of the trail.

From his use of the phrase "we formed ourselves" McClung himself must have been a member of the Independent Braves, but later, when he records actions taken by the group, he no longer uses "we", raising the possibility he may no longer have been a part of the group.

On the trip through what is now Nebraska and Eastern Wyoming, the Kennedy train travelers had seen, talked to and traded with many Indians; they had seen and visited many Indian villages along the way. While they had been cautioned about letting Indians into their encampments and guarded their property against theft, these were "good Indians" in the language of the day. After Independence Rock, they would see few Indian villages. The dwellings of the Indians were now somewhere else, out of sight of the overland trail.

Sarah Zaring Howard wrote about her memory of the Indians, friendly and not so friendly, in 1932. "One bright sunny day we came in sight of our first Indians. They were of the Pawnee tribe and friendly to the whites. They were dressed in native garb, and armed with bows and arrows, and out for a hunt....It was not long until we could see great camps or villages of Indians. I think there were hundreds of them in these camps. Their tents were made of the skins of animals and set very close together.

"As long as we were among friendly tribes, these camps were visible, but when we came to the country where we did not find the Indian camps, then we understood we were among hostile tribes. Whenever we camped near an Indian village, the Indians would come in droves to our camp to beg or barter for some of the white man's foods. Sometimes they would bring fish to get something in exchange..."

Interviewed at age 92, Christena Taylor Chambers takes a different slant. "Even friendly Indians could not always be trusted. The tribes were realizing finally that the whites were taking the country away from them and they were desperate." These were the Indians whose lands the Kennedy train would traverse, with no army troops to call on for protection, for the next 700 miles.

No Harm in Killing a Man

On July 5, Kennedy was prompted to organize his Independent Braves to deal with the real threat of hostile Indians. While he would eventually need them for that purpose, he needed them first just two days later, and for an entirely different purpose.

Hamilton Scott was one of a number who wrote about the murder, trial and punishment forever associated with Kennedy and the Kennedy train. His account is characteristically terse and raises a number of questions, most of which have never been answered. "July 6. Drove about twenty-five miles. No grass at noon. At four o'clock P.M. passed two trains camped who informed us of a murder committed near them today. Two men quarreled about a team, one shot the other, took his team and money. We traveled late, found no grass; cattle suffering for feed..."

On the following day, desperate for feed for their cattle, the wagon train started out at sunrise – about 5:00 AM – an unusually early start, looking for grass. Normally they had breakfast before starting, but not that day. They had to get the stock to grass. They found grass for their cattle and much more. "...traveled four or five miles and found grass on river bottom. Several trains were camped here so we drove in and camped too. We are informed that the murderer is camped here. By request of some men from another camp, Captain Kennedy of our train ordered out twenty men, well armed to surround and take him, which they did. With court organized and a jury of twelve men selected, he was given a fair trial and a twelve to one (sic) verdict, guilty of willful murder."

From other accounts we know that on Sunday, July 6, the day the Kennedy train left Independence Rock, a man named Young shot and killed his partner, George Scott (no relation to our diarist, Hamilton Scott). R. Young (full name unknown) and Scott were miners working in the Pike's Peak area of Colorado. They had heard of the discovery of gold in the Powder River area of Oregon and set out together for the new find. They pooled their resources and acquired the necessary provisions.

Some time before they reached Independence Rock, Young and Scott had a major falling out and a complete divorce in their partnership. They divided everything and continued on their separate ways. But Young wasn't satisfied with the division of property. Scott took property that belonged to him, Young believed. Particularly in question was the ownership of a team of horses. Brooding over the injustice of it all, Young decided to settle the matter himself.

James McClung describes Young's action in his diary entry that day: "(Young) slipped up behind Scott, shot him in the back with a double barreled shotgun, killing him immediately. Then, digging a hole, threw him in and drove on. When we came up, the grave had been opened by Pitman's train. The scene was an awful one. We dug the grave deeper and buried him in a respectable manner and drove several miles and camped on the Sweetwater. No grass."

While it seems Young (and Scott before he was murdered) was not a member of any wagon train, it was not unusual for individuals or small groups of wagons to travel and camp near larger groups of emigrants for protection. When the leaders of the small wagon trains camped by the Sweetwater realized the murderer was brazenly camped in their midst that evening, now in possession of his victim's horses, wagon, property and money, they were shocked and met together to decide what to do, or whether they should decide to do anything. They weren't organized for forceful action and could not agree on what to do. What they did, was spend a sleepless night worrying about the killer nearby.

The early morning arrival of the Kennedy train, 80 wagons strong, while the campers from the small trains were still eating their breakfasts, changed everything. The sheriff and the cavalry had arrived. Kennedy wasn't a sheriff, but he had been. The Independent Braves were not the cavalry, but the closest thing to it. Kennedy and his people seemed like the answer to the loose murderer problem and they went to him with a plea to do something .

Kennedy had sound reasons not to get involved. He had no legal jurisdiction to do anything of course; no one did. Moreover, neither Kennedy nor anyone from his train had witnessed the murder and he could reasonably argue the responsibility to deal with Young should go to others. Surely there must have been members of his train who would have argued just that. "It's not our problem. Let's stay out of it."

Kennedy had an even better reason not to get involved: the inherent difficulty of trial and punishment on the trail. Beyond the reach of legitimate law enforcement and courts, there was no way a trial could be held in accord with even the looser legal procedures of that time. Then the big problem: punishment. Once a guilty verdict was reached on the trail, there were only two possible punishments: banishment or execution. The alternative of prison was not available. In this case, banishment would mean nothing; Young was not a member of any of the wagon trains on the scene.

There were still some army units nearby. How about turning a murderer over to the army? Not possible. The army consistently refused to take custody of civilians accused of crimes, even when there were no civil authorities within hundreds of miles. They simply did not have that authority. Army veteran Kennedy understood that and he also must have well understood immediately, that if he agreed to the request he would have to try and execute the man.

Kennedy, knowing all that, didn't hesitate. He immediately agreed to take on the problem in their midst. It must have been about 8:00 AM that morning when, as Hamilton Scott recorded, Kennedy "ordered out twenty men to surround and take him." Scott's diary shows the verdict as "twelve to one". (Perhaps he meant eleven to one or twelve to none. No one else recorded the vote of the jury.)

McClung's account told us that Kennedy "called out the Independent Braves and took Mr. R. Young a prisoner and gave him a fair trial and was found guilty." Whether McClung himself participated, he doesn't say.

Others gave accounts of the trial many years later. Robert Cummins, voted Justice of Peace or Judge for the train wrote simply: "We were called on to arrest a man on a charge of murder, for which he was given a trial, convicted and executed." No information survives as to who presided at the trial. It probably was not Robert Cummins. He later wrote about the trial and execution without claiming that role. Had he presided, I believe Robert Cummins, would have said so. With only a basic education, Cummins had never served as a judge or justice of the peace prior to joining the Kennedy train, nor did he hold any such position afterwards.

Kennedy himself may have presided at the trial, though there is no evidence of it. Perhaps someone from one of the other small trains presided. That and many other important facts about the trial were omitted from the accounts of a number of people who recorded what they remembered about it.

A 1942 Walla Walla Union-Bulletin story reported the 92nd birthday recollections of Mary Elizabeth Paul Maxson. She was eleven years old at the time of the trip across the plains. "Justice was meted out to those causing trouble in the party. Mrs. Maxson recollects the train coming upon a man's body half-buried in a rocky grave and the pursuit of the murderer and his trial by jury. He was convicted and given his choice of death by hanging, drowning or a firing squad with the guilty one choosing the latter."

The same year, a Pomeroy, Washington newspaper recorded the memories of the event as told by Martha McGuire Fitzsimmons, who had been nine years old at the time. "Often the plains were marked with an occasional solitary mound with a slab of wood or a stone. One day some of the men in the party caught sight of a dead man half buried in the ground, feet sticking out. Murder was immediately suspicioned, and a man known to be a hard character was suspected. A group went ahead and arrested the fellow and he was brought back, tried and convicted..."

Another Kennedy train survivor, Christena Taylor Chambers was only five in 1862, but her 1950 account of the murder trial, told to the Portland Oregonian in 1950 is the only known account which tells anything at all about the trial itself. "On July 6 there was a murder. Two men with a mule team had joined the train, the younger man shot the little old man who owned the outfit but did not get him buried before the train came up.

"A jury of 12 men assembled in a rough enclosure of logs. A fire was kept going, and the accused man was there under guard. Children clambered on logs and others drew near and listened. The sentence was death by shooting. The man had little to say for himself except that he didn't know there was any harm in killing a man on the plains. He had a family back east and spent most of the night writing letters...."

We might question Chambers' total recall of the trial and Young's testimony, an event occurring when she was five years old. Perhaps she remembered her parents telling her the details of what was an important event in her life. Her description of the trial certainly sounds like a true account of someone who was there. Also, her recollection of the murderer's testimony squares very neatly with Young's brazen actions after the killing. Young seems to have been well-versed in the belief that there was no law on the plains and it was nobody's business that he had killed a man.

While Mrs. Chambers' account gives us a good picture of the event, neither her account nor any of the others answers the obvious questions about it. One thing we do know: the trial didn't last very long. It was all over by 2:00 PM. Scott wrote: "The prisoner kept under guard, we hitched up at two PM and drove eight miles. Grass and water good." The Kennedy train had not arrived in the area where the murderer was camping until about 8:00 AM. After that, they had to capture Young, select a jury and make arrangements for the trial. The trial itself couldn't have lasted more than two or three hours, perhaps less.

The accounts we have of the trial leave many questions. How was the court organized? Who presided? How was the jury selected? Did Young have a defense counsel? Perhaps he did. Hamilton Scott's brother, Robert Scott, writing about the trial later added to Hamilton's account the fact that "They formed a court, a judge, lawyers and 12 jury men..." Did Young testify, as Christena Chambers recalled? In Hamilton Scott's diary he refers to a twelve to one verdict, perhaps an inadvertent mistake. Among the members of the Kennedy train were there those who disagreed with Kennedy's decision to take on the responsibility of what to do with a murderer on the plains?

We could look at Kennedy's decision to take responsibility for Young and ask 'what else could he have done?' Perhaps it was just the right thing to do and there was no reason to hesitate or confer with others about the decision. It seems that way now, looking at Kennedy's action nearly a century and a half later. But that would ignore how rare Kennedy's action was in the history of the overland trail. Of the many murders that must have occurred during the period of the western-bound wagon trains, how many resulted in a trial and punishment on the trail? David J. Langum, in his article "Pioneer Justice on the Overland Trail" tells us. Only five.

Langum says "(only) the Lafayette Tate trial and a few other examples of trial for murder on the plains were serious efforts at judicial action, in which calm deliberation was combined with real punishment..." He lists five; Lafayette Tate, June 15, 1852; James Tooly, August 1857; George W. Hickey, September 5, 1849; Leandas Balsley, June 15, 1852; and "an unnamed assailant of July 6, 1862". The "unnamed assailant" was R. Young, executed by the Kennedy Company. He quotes Randall A. Hewitt, "Across the Plains and Over the Divide". "Yesterday passed the grave of a man murdered on the 6th instant. Today we passed the tomb of the murderer. He was caught, tried and shot the next day. Retribution in this case (was) speedy and summary. The tedious, tardy and too often doubtful manner of administering what is termed "justice" in the States, had few admirers on the plains."

In another account by Randall A. Hewitt, he repeats the story with other details. "...A paper tacked to a headboard detailed the story of his pursuit, capture, trial and death by shooting. He had been followed by men of his party, caught, a trial by jury summoned from among other emigrant trains and his guilt being established, his condemnation and death followed promptly. Retribution was summary....This murderer, after being condemned, was blindfolded and led to the grave prepared for him and shot by a squad of his fellow pilgrims."

Although Hewitt failed to record the name of the murderer, the event described was of the trial, conviction and execution of R. Young by the Kennedy train on July 7 and 8, 1862. On a reading of approximately 200 overland diaries and reminiscences, Langum could find only five examples of trials and punishment carried out on the overland trail. "Only in the relatively rare situation of deliberate murder, did the pioneers ever unite in a calm manner to effectuate judicial deliberation and punishment." Rare as it was, this is exactly what the Kennedy train did on July 7 and 8, 1862.

Can it be Possible?

While the court convened by Kennedy had promptly found the prisoner guilty of "willful murder", neither Scott nor McClung mentioned a decision by the court as to what punishment was to be assessed. That issue was left for later. It had been comparatively easy to organize a court and reach a verdict of guilt in a trial, and it was a process of which all of the emigrants were familiar. Most had participated in or witnessed trials back home. Probably very few had participated in or witnessed an execution, yet that was the next step after finding Young guilty.

From McClung's diary, we get his opinion of what Kennedy had in mind when, prisoner in tow, he got the train underway at 2:00 PM. "...we then traveled on expecting to deliver him into the hands of the soldiers. So towards night we camped near a company of (the 6th) Ohio cavalry. Captain Greg and several others from Laramie was present tonight but as they were not present at the trial, said they had no right to punish him but it was Kennedy's place."

Did Kennedy believe the army would take the convicted man off his hands and see to his punishment? That is what McClung says, but Kennedy had served as an army 1st Sergeant on the overland trail as a teamster for military wagon trains. He had been a county sheriff in Iowa. Kennedy must have known the army would not take jurisdiction. He must have known he would have to execute the murderer himself.

Kennedy traveled to the army detachment to get the support of the commanding officer for the execution. If that was Kennedy's aim, he more than succeeded. He not only got the agreement of the captain that it was "Kennedy's place" to punish Young, he also persuaded the army officer to participate in the execution.

He must have known he would have to face criticism from some for executing the man, so he proceeded with caution to line up support for the action. He put it to a vote of the whole company, per McClung's account. "He then put it to a vote what should be done with the prisoner and was carried by a large majority in favor of his death." His is the only account of the vote, but it appears there were dissenters in the company who didn't agree with the "large majority" who favored his death. Who they were and what they would have done with Young, we don't know.

Now with a nod from the army captain and a vote of the whole company to back him up, Kennedy prepared for the execution, scheduled for 8:00 AM the following day, Tuesday, July 8. First he needed a firing squad and he had one, the Independent Braves, which he had organized just three days before. Second, he wanted a show of evidence of the army's approval of the execution. From McClung we learn Kennedy had arranged for the army captain to take command of his 25 Independent Braves and the captain escorted the prisoner to the place of execution. The legitimacy of the execution was now backed up by the United States Army, or at least by one officer of that army.

Western historian John Phillip Reid cites the 25 man firing squad employed by Kennedy as "...what seems to be the largest firing squad in the history of the overland trail." Another western historian, Merrill Mattes comments that "it is somewhat remarkable that Kennedy could find so many executioners. It was reported in 1849 that a man convicted of murder had to be released because no one could be found to execute him." Kennedy apparently had no difficulty turning out his Independent Braves in force for the execution.

The same people who wrote or told about the trial also reported on the execution, with some variation in details. Young James McClung reported the execution in the most complete and emotional detail. While he was, or had been a member of the Independent Braves, there is nothing in his narrative to indicate he himself pointed a rifle and fired a shot into the convicted man. Perhaps he was part of the execution squad but didn't want to say so. However, his account certainly seems to be from a witness, not a participant.

Witness or participant, McClung seems to have been emotionally moved by the incident.

"They gave him till morning to dispose of his property and prepare for the other world. What a solemn thought. 'Can it be possible' said he. With that the tear drops fell from his eyes like showers of rain. A person named Stephan Hill was appointed to do his writing and prayed and talked with him till morning....It was a calm, still morning and a day to be long remembered. He picked the spot himself on the bank of the little Sweetwater, where he was to be laid in the mother earth.

"At eight o'clock was the hour of execution. The time slowly passed on. He had his choice to be hung or shot. In choosing to be shot, he was placed in a high seat between two other persons on a four horse wagon. Our Captain then called out the company of Independent Braves. Captain Greg took command and escorted the prisoner to the place of execution, where Captain Kennedy again took charge of the company. They gave him 15 minutes to talk, when the tears again fell like rain, as they held the watch and told him the time. As it passed, he talked a few words privately. When 10 minutes had passed, he knelt down in secret prayer and when the 5 minutes was out he raised to his feet and was marched out in line with the company.

"After going some 10 paces, they halted and turned back leaving him in a position about half bent and with his face inclined toward the sun, with a handkerchief in his hand, and weeping like a child, Kennedy giving the orders to fire, the prisoner fell dead in the presence of a thousand people. No one moved, but held their breath. The weight of a pin might have been heard fall on the ground. The scene was awful. He was then buried in order, the company firing over the grave. The large sympathizing audience heard the echo die away in the forest and all was still.

"The tears could be seen in the eyes of many as they left the grave of the deceased, which lies tonight on the bank of the little Sweetwater in the Rattlesnake Mountains." McClung ends his entry for that day, July 8,1862, with the remainder of the day's events. "From here we traveled 12 miles and camped on Sweetwater and swum the cattle across the river where we found pretty good grass. The weather was good." The trial and execution of Young had cost the Kennedy train little time. They covered 13 or 14 miles on the day of the trial and 12 miles on the day of the execution, just a little less than the usual 15 or 20 miles. It was a busy two days.

McClung's account reveals something like genuine sympathy for the condemned man, from McClung himself as well as from the "large sympathizing audience", many of whom shed tears. Just as Young asked 'could it be possible' many in the crowd must have asked themselves, can it be possible we are going to execute a man? They watched a sight they had never seen before and would never see again. They never forgot it. They remembered the execution for the remainder of their lives. Many wrote or told about the event decades later. While others commented about the emotional impact of seeing the execution, none of the Kennedy company ever questioned the appropriateness of the action Kennedy took.

Not only was the Young execution carried out with the largest firing squad in overland trail history, the execution was likely witnessed by the largest audience in trail history. If McClung's estimate of 1000 witnesses to the execution is correct, in addition to the 300 or so members of the Kennedy party, there must have been more than twice that number there from other trains.

Scott's diary entry about the execution displays his more emotionally reserved character. "Captain Kennedy called their whole company together and laid the case before them. They decided that the prisoner be executed tomorrow morning... Gave prisoner his choice to be shot or hanged. He preferred to be shot. Twenty-five armed men marched him one-half mile to where his grave had been prepared. Fourteen of the guns were loaded with bullets and the rest were blanks. When the signal was given, they all fired, the prisoner falling backwards and dying within one minute. It was a sad sight to look upon. We immediately laid him in his grave without even a rough box. As soon as our work was completed, we moved on toward the setting sun."

Watching the execution as children created a vivid and moving memory on those who later recalled it. When she was 92, Mary Elizabeth Paul Maxon told a newspaper reporter there were two things she would never forget: "the prisoner's cries all through the night and the sight of him sitting on his coffin facing the firing squad and his subsequent fall as the fatal shot was fired.

Martha McGuire Fitzsimmons recalled "They led him off to shoot him out of sight of the women and children. I recall seeing the poor fellow taken away."

Some of the details remembered by Christena Taylor Chambers, five years old during the crossing, differ from other accounts. "In the morning, the oxen were yoked and the train prepared to move. A firing squad of 12 men was ready, some of the rifles carrying blank loads. A grave had been dug and a coffin made of boards from the decking of a wagon. The man sat on the coffin and waited. (My) father, face white, held the horns of his oxen to keep them from stampeding. I can hear those guns yet."

Woodson Cummins, son of Robert Cummins, judge or justice of the peace on the Kennedy train celebrated his seventh birthday on July 6, 1862, the day of the murder. In his later years he talked often about his experience on the wagon train, to me and several of his other grandchildren. Mostly he talked about the execution, his chief memory of the trip. His story of the execution included the information that the prisoner had to dig his own grave. No one else remembered that. In his account, he watched the execution by peeking under the wagon canvas, after being told not to look, by his parents. Since other accounts place the execution well away from the wagon train – a half mile according to Scott – perhaps Woodson's memory of the event was not perfect.

One thing stands out. None of the accounts from Kennedy's train criticized him for capturing, trying and executing Young, even though his action was completely extra-legal. Even after the completion of the trip when James McClung wrote a letter home to Iowa severely criticizing Kennedy's actions during the trip, he was completely silent about the execution of Young. Perhaps those of the "large majority" who voted to execute Young remembered their assent to the execution and were not in a position later to criticize it. Or, perhaps the execution seemed so obviously proper under the circumstances, they never thought to question it.

Still, Kennedy didn't escape criticism, not from his own company, but from Jane Gould, a member of another wagon train. A number of different wagon trains crossed and re-crossed paths. Trains often camped or stopped at noon near other trains and the travelers visited with each other and compared experiences. Twenty days after the execution, July 28, 1862, Jane Gould's wagon train encountered the Kennedy train. It was a time when Kennedy and his train were facing a number of serious difficulties.

She listed the various problems – deaths and stampedes - and added "They seem to be very unfortunate. It is the Kennedy train." Six days later Jane Gould added "The Captain of this Canady or Kennedy train is the man who arrested Young (that murdered Scott) and ordered him to be shot. He did not belong to this train but to another. Some say that it is a judgment upon him and his train for meddling with and depriving a man of his life without the aid of the law. After cattle have been frightened once of twice, there is no safety with them. Yesterday there were several loose horses came running up when the whole train of cattle started pell-mell, crippled two men besides killing the woman. They mark nearly half their camps with dead cattle. I never supposed that cattle would run so in the yoke and hitched to the wagon."

If Jane Gould disapproved of Kennedy's acting "without the aid of the law", the previously quoted Randall A. Hewitt, who traveled past the two graves later, gave a ringing endorsement to Kennedy as a model worthy of emulation and noted "The tedious, tardy and too often doubtful manner of what is termed 'justice' in the States, has few admirers on the plains." No, Kennedy's actions could definitely not be characterized as 'tedious', 'tardy' or 'doubtful'.

From Hewitt's comments it seems that arguments about due process and court delays are not just a modern phenomenon.

As Jane Gould pointed out, Kennedy's actions deprived a murderer of his life and the "aid of the law" was absent. There simply was no law to aid Kennedy on the trail along the Sweetwater in what is now Wyoming. It was not at all strange to members of Kennedy's train that their captain acted to try, convict and execute a murderer near them. They had elected to travel with a man of action ready and willing to take prompt and decisive action and Kennedy didn't disappoint them. Members of the Kennedy train viewed themselves as part of a legitimate governmental entity. Moreover, their vote for execution made them all accomplices.

It was not uncommon at the time to attribute reverses and disasters to divine judgment as members of Jane Gould's train did. As members of the Kennedy train dealt with the tribulations they were to have later in the trip, perhaps some of them also attributed their reverses to divine judgment.

Reading what we now have about Young's trial and execution leaves many unanswered questions. If we could only bring back young James McClung and Hamilton Scott, there are many questions they could answer. For example, why did Kennedy and the Kennedy train get involved with the trial and execution of Young? Some of the other trains were closer to the murder, maybe even eye witnesses to the event.

While it is only conjecture, they would probably explain that everybody knew about Captain John K. Kennedy. They knew he was a sheriff and they knew how well organized the train was, even with its own militia. They may also have noted that the people in the small trains were afraid of the murderer. Anyone who would commit such a flagrant crime was not someone to be talked to and reasoned with.

Answers to still other questions remain uncertain. Why did Kennedy take Young to the army detachment when it was unlikely the army would take jurisdiction? Also, who voted on the question of executing Young? Was it just the Kennedy train, or did all of the thousand emigrants assembled have a voice in the decision?

James McClung wrote a very moving account of the execution, indicating some sympathy for Young. I wish I could have asked him how it happened that he was not among the 25 executioners. He was a member of the Independent Braves, who escorted Young to the execution spot, yet his account of the event is that of a witness, not of a participant. Perhaps Kennedy asked for volunteers and McClung did not volunteer or was not selected.

Hard on the Stock and Trying on the Women

The location Young picked for his grave along the Sweetwater is near the present site of Jeffry City in central Wyoming. As the Kennedy train headed west from the execution site on July 8, the company faced ten days and 130 miles of rugged travel across the Continental Divide before reaching the Green River, then at flood stage. The altitude at Jeffry City is about 6500 feet; the westward trail rises to about 7500 feet at South Pass on the Continental Divide, then drops down to about 4500 feet at Marbleton, in Western Wyoming near where the party reached the Green River.

Although they crossed this part of the trail during the hottest time of the year, in July 1862 the area was still recovering from an unusually heavy snowfall and cold winter and spring. While some days were hot, they found deep snowdrifts along the trail and frozen springs. Some mornings they woke up to white frost on the ground.

The Kennedy train suffered no serious setbacks during that ten day period. No Indian troubles; no stampedes, no murderers lurking about; just the usual difficulties the emigrants had to face surviving the day to day hardships of wagon train travel, problems that largely fell on the women.

One of James McClung's entries during this part of the trip commented that wagon train travel was "very hard on our stock and trying on the women and children." Decades later, several of the women from the Kennedy train described the day to day living arrangements, largely omitted from the diaries of the young bachelors, Hamilton Scott and James McClung.

Ellen Paul Garlington, age nine during the trip described the food. "Our food was very plain. We could not take fresh vegetables as they were so perishable. Canned fruit and vegetables were then unknown. The fare was mostly meat and bread made of white flour mixed with salt and water and baked. Milk thickened with flour was a standby and of course it was nourishing and easily prepared. It was usually the evening meal.

"Riding in heavy wagons on the rough trail was very tiresome. In the mornings the children used to like to walk ahead of the train, sometimes for hours at a time, until quite tired out. Then the riding did not seem so bad. Roads were mainly deep ruts, at the time of year very dusty."

Mary Elizabeth Paul Maxson, age eleven at the time, later supplied the information that "each wagon was equipped with a loaded gun and ammunition". She also explained how the cows provided both food and motive power. "(We) brought two milk cows which, incidentally worked with the oxen the while furnishing plenty of milk and butter, the churning done enroute by the motion of the rough riding wagons...The train stopped every Saturday but three, when water was not available. Repairs were made, washing and baking were done in preparation for the next week's journey".

Martha McGuire Fitzsimmons, age 10 at the time remembered the monotony of the trip. "It took six months to reach Walla Walla...day after day, week after week, month after month there was nothing but sagebrush, greasewood and prairie sand. We would sleep, ride and walk again and again, for miles and miles." She also provided details of the way things were done on the trail. "We hungered for fresh fruit and vegetables, and used to eat the buds or seed pods of wild roses...The food carried by the emigrants consisted mostly of bacon, flour, home-made sorghum syrup and coffee. There was no butter, no jam, no canned goods. They cooked on sheet iron stoves, baked by use of reflectors and burned sagebrush and buffalo chips.

"In camping, the wagons were placed in a circle and the emigrants and cattle were placed inside, with men on guard at night....Once in a while one of the cattle died along the way, making it necessary to leave buggies, hacks, saddles or furniture, when draft power of the remaining animals became so depleted that these could not be taken."

More details were provided by Christena Taylor Chambers. "Cows were brought along. Cream in a crock in the wagon made butter during a day's jolting. Hot biscuits were baked almost every morning in a reflector oven. Raised bread was baked when a stop was made for clothes washing. There always was food for all..." She added, "On through September the weary caravan went on. Lots of people wished they'd never come."

In 1926 Margaret Stoot Theil provided more detail in her interview with a Walla Walla newspaper. She had been sixteen at the time of the trip and traveled with her mother and step-father, John K. Kennedy. "Before leaving Iowa, my stepfather had bought four riding horses and four side-saddles for myself and my sisters. We would ride ahead of the train, select a camping place and gather wood or buffalo chips and, by the time the wagon train had caught up with us, we had the campfires going. Our horses died on the plains and as the cattle were getting gaunt and weak, my stepfather wouldn't let us put the side-saddles in the wagon. I carried my side saddle two days before I finally abandoned it by the side of the road."

She also told of running out of food. "Instead of being four months on the road, we were six months. There were nine in our family besides the hired man. Traveling on foot and being out in the open all the time gives you a big appetite, so the first thing we knew, we were out of coffee, sugar, bacon, tea, and flour."

The first day on the road after Young's execution, James McClung's diary entry gives us an idea of his state of mind, enjoying the wildness of the country around him, as well as a vivid description of what he was seeing. "July 9th...This is a desolate looking part of the world. We are plum out of civilization in a land inhabited by nothing but the wild beasts of the forest and the red men that is seeking an opportunity to destroy us and take our property. But not one of them is visible, although their footprints are many in the sand and their war paths are beaten smooth. However, we keep the company out and scouting parties all the time.

"About the middle of the afternoon, which was very warm, I came to one of the prettiest springs I ever saw where water raised up above the surface but soon lost itself again in the sand among the sagebrush and, I being very thirsty, I was induced to taste it and being in a hurry to taste it and get a cool drink, but when my lips touched the water, I was scared and very much disappointed in finding it was boiling hot. This was a curiosity to us all..."

Since none of the women on the Kennedy train are known to have kept a diary of the trip, we are left to rely on the diaries of the two young bachelors, Hamilton Scott and James McClung and, except for the recollections a few provided in their later years, we do not get a picture of what the women of the party would have said about events, or how they would have described what they saw and experienced. We do however have Jane Gould's diary written the same year.

For the most part, the daily journeys of Jane Gould's wagon train do not coincide with the Kennedy train, but for the ten day period from the execution site to the Green River, the day by day journeys are a close match, Gould's train about three days behind Kennedy's. Starting July 8 for Kennedy's train and July 11 for Gould's, the two trains cover much the same ground. It is interesting to compare what the young men saw and wrote and match their accounts with Jane Gould's.

On July 12 Jane Gould's journey covered the same ground McClung had described above on July 9 as a "desolate looking part of the world". Jane's account in part reads "Found no feed for our cattle at noon but we stopped long enough to eat lunch and for the men to exchange some pork for beef with soldiers who are stationed nearby. Mr. Church has a very sick ox. Is obliged to yoke his cow with an ox...We passed by an ice springs. The Captain dug down a few inches and they got a pail of Ice on the 12th of July..." McClung had found a hot spring; Gould an ice spring.

On the following day, Hamilton Scott tells us there were "about 200 wagons camped here and some soldiers who protect the emigrants". Gould's diary for the matching day tells us what the women were doing. "Did not travel today but washed, baked, cooked beef, stewed peaches, boiled corn. We had an excellent feed, the best we have had for some time. There were several soldiers came to call on us..."

McClung that day saw something much different, a dog waiting by a grave. "On top of the hill we passed a grave. The inscription on the head-board read as follows: 'Two persons named Megraw who was brother-in-laws was killed by the Indians on the 29th of June, 1862'...at the head of the grave lay their favorite dog which was almost starved to death. I tried to coax him to go with me but all in vain. In giving him provisions enough for several days, I left him lying by the grave."

On the next day, July 11th for Scott and McClung, Hamilton Scott notes that they "camped close to a large snow bank". McClung noted the "dust, which is four inches deep, makes it very uncomfortable on the women and children that is compelled to walk as their teams is growing thin." For the matching day Jane Gould tells us "There were some soldiers stationed near us. We gave them a pail of milk."

On July 12, Scott notes they stayed in camp to set "wagon tires, and shoeing cattle, etc." McClung's report of activities is more comprehensive, if not completely clear. "We lay by for the purpose of resting our cattle, repairing wagons, shoeing cattle and the women have to wash and cook. Fixing to travel makes it very hard on them from the fact they never have no time to rest." Just who it was that had "no time to rest" is vague. Was it the cattle, the women or both? On the matching day, July 15 for Gould, she notices the altitude, now over 7000 feet and looks at the scenery. "We are getting to such an altitude that the air is quite rare and I, for one, feel rather more lazy than usual.... We came in sight of Table Rock this afternoon."

On the 13th both Scott and McClung note that they are now on the Landers Cutoff; Gould doesn't mention it, but does smell the flowers on the 16th, when her wagon train took the same fork in the trail to the north near the continental divide. Her entry in part that day: "Did some baking...We find several kinds of very pretty flowers, a number of kinds of mosses. One has a pretty white flower and is very fragrant like the fragrance of the grass pink."

McClung explains about the Landers Cutoff with some anxiety. "In leaving the main road we soon learned that the Landers Cutoff was new and had never been traveled a great deal...we are now on the summit of the Rocky Mountains, where the waters run towards the Pacific Ocean." He had reason for some anxiety. The Cutoff had been built by the government under the direction of Frederick Landers in 1858 and shortened the trip to California or Oregon by 60 miles. It followed an old Indian trail well to the north of the main trail. There were advantages and disadvantages, but when the 1862 trains reached the part of the Cutoff ascending the Salt River Range, in what is now Western Wyoming, they found much of the road gone, washed out by the unusually high snow runoff the previous winter and spring. It was little used after 1862. Today, what was the route of the Landers Cutoff through the mountains west from Big Piney, Wyoming is an unimproved winding gravel road, Wyoming highway #350.

Relying only on Jane Gould's accounts, we would not know about the Landers Cutoff, or about crossing the Continental Divide or about the dog guarding the grave of his master, killed by Indians. Relying only on the diaries of the two young bachelors, we would not have known there were fragrant flowers along the trail or known of the rarity of oxygen or known what kind of food the emigrants were eating. Fortunately, for part of the trip, we have them both.

On July 14, James McClung wrote "Lay in camp for a day. Something like 50 teams passed us today." Scott confirms they did not travel and tells us why. "E. E. Ellis' wife brought a newcomer into camp last night." The baby Eliza Jane Ellis had been carrying since the beginning of the trip three months earlier had arrived. She was one of two women who started on the journey in Iowa in April six months pregnant. Apparently everything went well and the decision to undertake the cross-country wagon train did not turn out to be a mistake for the Ellis E. Ellis family. No other details are known. The wagon train resumed the move west the following day.

Starting the trip, James McClung recorded some reasons why he wanted to take the trip west, including a desire to "see the snow capped mountains...chase the antelope... and see the grizzly bear." On July 15, 1862 some of those hopes were realized; also a little adventure and danger, which he records with just a hint of breathlessness.

"...After dinner a small company of us went hunting and killed three antelopes. Here we seen some elk and something we supposed to be a small herd of buffalos at several miles distant. In climbing a high mountain which was covered with as beautiful timber which ever grew from (100) to 200 feet high where the ground was covered with snow from one to ten feet deep. In looking about, I seen a fresh grizzly track and in following it there were several tracks that resembled Indians. Finally they became more numerous...In seeing they were in pursuit of the bear, I stopped to rest and, thinking I was alone and six miles from camp and among hostile Indians and it getting late, I started for camp.

"I passed several wigwams where the smoke was coming out through a hole in the top. They were located on the bank of one fork in the Sweetwater, in the timber about five miles from the road. Knowing if I should be seen by them my cake would be all (done?), I cautiously slipped by with my gun and revolver both cocked in order to be ready for the emergency at any moment. I, however, passed in safety and reached camp about dark, somewhat tired and hungry, having traveled about 15 miles."

It's impossible to know whether McClung's fear of hostile Indians was justified, though the experience of the Kennedy train later in the trip would argue that it was. Even if the Indians he saw were of the friendly type, McClung certainly seems to have been in plenty of danger hiking through the wilderness all alone, miles from his camp with his "gun and revolver both cocked." McClung's unquestioning account of this part of his adventure seems to bear out the fact that many of those rough and ready emigrants, including McClung, were still greenhorns, members of a train of innocents.

On the same day McClung went out on his hunting adventure, Hamilton Scott seems to have stayed home but still benefited from the hunt. "Some of the men shot an antelope which seems to be the best meat I've ever eaten."

Three days later near the location of McClung's hunt, Jane Gould reported: "When we arose this morning there was a heavy white frost on the ground. It seemed cold enough to be winter. I don't see how anything can grow here...The road is quite good, [better than] we supposed it would be crossing the Rocky Mountains...The men found two or three good wagons, some harnesses, scythes, a stove...in a ravine off half-a-mile from the road...we found several kinds of new flowers..."

On July 16 McClung told us "...we passed over high rocky peaks, which were very hard on our

stock and trying on the women and children..."
Could there be a pattern here? We could read too
much into it, but McClung does have a tendency
to comment on the hardships faced by the oxen
and the women, both in the same sentence. He
also wrote that day about crossing the Big Sandy
River which he judged "cold enough to freeze a
man to death". At the same location, three days
later, Jane Gould "saw this morning the Green
River Mountains for the first time." Perhaps she
was seeing what is now on maps as the Wyoming
Range.

On July 17 the Kennedy train arrived at the crossing
point of what was then called the Green River,
now called the New Fork River, ending the calm
before the storm represented by the past ten days
traveling over the continental divide from the site
of Young's execution. Scott's diary was terse: "...to
Green River where we camped, it being dark."
McClung reported: "...cold and drizzling and very
disagreeable...on reaching the Green River at nine
PM, here was hundreds of emigrants camped and
making preparation for crossing next day...I stood
guard half the night."

Jane Gould arrived at the Green River crossing
point three days later, at three PM, July 20 and
gave an account of a pleasant evening. "Here
the feed was not good but better than none...the
timber I think is elm. The men had a ball play
towards night; seemed to enjoy themselves. It
seemed like old times." She also gave a partial

picture of the problem the trains were having getting over the river. "The Captain sent a man down to a ferry that was ten miles below us on the river to see about crossing. The charge was four dollars per wagon and swim our own cattle and have to wait our turn to cross." Apparently the cost of the crossing and the likely long wait for the ferry caused Jane Gould's train to seek other methods of crossing the raging river, because the following day "our men went to work this morning to build a raft..."

A Dangerous Undertaking

All the wagon trains arriving at the regular Green River crossing point faced a problem they had not expected. They had expected to ferry their wagons across, but there was no ferry. Due to the unusually high water at the crossing point, the only available ferry was ten miles away, with perhaps a delay of several days and a charge of four dollars per wagon. The Kennedy train faced a major challenge which could have become a disaster. Other trains that year lost lives and wagons at the same crossing. James McClung, Hamilton Scott and others explained how they managed to cross.

McClung's entries for July 18 and 19 follow: "Some of us went to hunt grass while others was making arrangements about crossing the river which is very swift and tolerable high. As there was no ferry boat and no way of crossing, only fastening three wagons back together, so we set in to work and by noon we had two boats constructed. We succeeded in ferrying across several wagons against dark. It is very slow work as every wagon has to be unloaded from the bank. We can only take across a little at a time, by taking the wagons apart we manage to get them across."

On the 19th, "We succeeded in all getting across by dark but had considerable trouble in swimming our stock. However we got them all across safe notwithstanding it is a dangerous stream for I saw several that had their teams drowned there, and out of one train a few days ago there was two men drowned here in swimming a horse across."

Scott added information about getting the stock across. "Swam our stock over this morning (July 19) and by dark we had the wagons all over safe without mishaps. The river was very high and running very rapid. We had considerable trouble in swimming our stock over. We put our horses in three at a time and they would go about half way across then turn downstream and drift back to the same side that we put them in on. We finally had to lead one beside our new constructed boats and the rest followed after him. It seemed almost a miracle that we got safely across."

Ellen Paul Garlington gave us a clearer and more vivid description of the process of getting the wagons, stock and people across the raging river. "The beautiful Green River was clear and deep and wide. On seeing it, our first thought was how we could ever get across. It was decided to make boats of the wagons, which were taken apart, rags and rosin were used to caulk them so they would be water tight. This was such a slow and awkward means of crossing it required three days to complete and get wagons ready to travel again. It was a comical sight, the men trying to paddle these queer looking crafts, and it provided much amusement for the youngsters after strenuous days of travel.

"Hardest task was to get the cattle started over. We drove them to the bank and every man, woman and child waved branches and pushed and shouted till finally the foremost horses and cows started into the water. After that, it was easy for the others followed and it was a beautiful sight to see them swimming across the wide river."

Sarah Zaring Howard remembered the crossing as "a very dangerous undertaking". "Our people crossed Green River in their wagon boxes, there being no ferry boat. Everything had to be unloaded from the wagons and the boxes made water-tight. The wagons were taken to pieces and all loaded into the boxes and long ropes fastened to them so they could be pulled ashore. It was a very dangerous undertaking however, and we didn't have a very good feeling until all were safely on the opposite side of the river."

Jane Gould's diary, writing about her crossing three days later, gives us a little more information about how the wagons were made into boats. "...Had to take them apart and float the box and the cover behind. The two boxes were fastened together by the rods, one before to row in and the other to load..."

The whole operation seems almost super-human. In two and a-half days, the Kennedy train had emptied all of something like 80 wagons, attached some of the wagon boxes together to make water-tight boats, disassembled all of the remaining wagons, then loaded all of the wagon parts and baggage into the newly constructed boats, then rowed everything to the other side of the swift river. On the other side, they completely reversed the process, put everything back together until it looked like a wagon train again and continued their trip west at noon on the third day. Kennedy's part in managing what seems like an incredible feat is not mentioned in any of the accounts, but surely he should have gotten some of the credit for such a successful operation. Not so.

There must have been some serious dissension in the Kennedy train during the crossing, not mentioned by anyone. James McClung's diary for July 20, the day the company completed the operation and started on the trail again, tells us all we know about the result of that dissension. "Some of the company falling out with Captain Kennedy as he was never satisfied and always finding fault in the company. Fifteen wagons seceded from his company and traveled on leaving us behind."

Something about the actions Kennedy took getting the wagon train across the flooded river must have alienated at least fifteen heads of families enough to cause them to invoke the "inalienable privilege of dissent", noted by DeVoto, prompting them to set out on their own. What Kennedy said or did, we don't know, but it would seem there must have been something more than "finding fault" to prompt the departure of the fifteen wagons.

While it's obvious McClung sides with the defectors, he and his party stayed with Kennedy, perhaps influencing him to mute his written criticism of Kennedy. However, for fifteen wagons to leave the safety of the large Kennedy train, indicates a serious rift in the company. This was the first, but not the last evidence of dissension on the Kennedy train.

We later learn that the leader of the defectors was one Ed Culberson (McClung's spelling). While McClung tells us why they seceded, "always finding fault", too bad we aren't able to directly ask Ed Culberson himself. While McClung may have been right, there are other factors which may have influenced the defectors. An 80 wagon train was slow and cumbersome. Perhaps they saw other smaller trains making better time and were willing to accept the supposed added danger of Indian attack on small trains. After all there had been no Indian problems up to that time.

Kennedy also may have had something to say about why the Culberson group set out on their own. Perhaps he would have told us that the defectors were contrary and uncooperative with his efforts at organizing the crossing of the Green River and yes, he did have cross words with those folks and good riddance.

Indians Attacking Around Here

The Kennedy train completed the crossing and reassembling of the wagons on July 20 and Scott told about the remainder of that day. "We hitched up the rest of the teams and drove six miles, camping on a branch of the Green River. We will have to ferry this, the same as the other river." That must have been a discouraging prospect for the train to face. Then, on the following day, July 21, good news. "There was an emigrant ferry boat found yesterday evening which our company bought for five dollars. Will get possession of it at three o'clock this evening..."

Jane Gould, arriving at the same place three days later discusses the buying and selling of ferry boats. "We got the use of the boat in time to bring over fourteen wagons tonight. The boat is an old scow. It is large enough to take a wagon and load over... Each train pays four dollars for it and the last man sells it to the next one back, so they all get their pay till it comes to the last train, who will be the loser of four dollars." The old scow Jane Gould's train bought for $4.00 was probably the same one the Kennedy train had purchased three days earlier for $5.00. It appears the Kennedy train paid a premium. If Jane Gould's explanation was correct, someone made a dollar profit off the Kennedy train.

James McClung's diary gives us more information about the crossing of what he calls the west fork of the Green River, now designated on maps simply as the Green River; also some information about the "seceders". "In six miles we came to the west fork of the Green River. Here we found quite a number of trains. Among the rest was the seceders. By this time they had elected the Rev. William E. Culberson their captain. He had acted as a lieutenant orderly in our train. He is a man who is respected and esteemed by all who are acquainted with him." One of the elected officers of the Kennedy train and fourteen other families had struck out on their own, hundreds of miles from the safety of military presence.

As a young single man, McClung must have attached himself to one of the emigrant families, trading his labor for a place in the wagon train. Most wagon parties included at least two men, the head of household and another relative, friend, or hired man. The work of handling the wagon and stock required it. That was the usual arrangement, although McClung never mentions who he was with. From his praise of Culberson, it's clear, McClung would have preferred escaping the Kennedy train and going with the "seceders", but he was probably committed to a wagon household who preferred to stay with Kennedy.

McClung's July 21 account describes the crossing of the second fork of the Green River on the scow. "...It was large enough to cross one wagon at a time with safety...this fork is something over 50 yards wide and very deep...By the middle of the afternoon the company was all across, then we ferried our wagons and against dark, swimming our stock."

Both forks of the Green River behind them, on July 22 the company heads west again. Scott's entry for the day follows: "All ferried over by ten o'clock ....We drove about ten miles this evening and camped on a creek. Saw some squads of Indians at a distance. We put out picket guards tonight. The Indians have been attacking the emigrants and stealing stock along here. They killed one man a day or two ago. His grave is close by our camp tonight." Many years later, Alvin Zaring, who traveled with Hamilton Scott, noted that when they passed by the grave, "his little dog was lying on the lonely grave." For the second time, someone on the train has seen a dog waiting on his master's grave, the master killed by Indians.

James McClung's July 22 entry reports an incident not mentioned by Scott. "...Some Mormon gurrillaes (sic) pretending to be in pursuit of some Indians that had stolen some stock at Fort Bridger, came riding up, some in front and some in the rear, and others passing through the middle of the train. We suspected them and the company got their guns and fell into line and the gairrillaes (sic) scattered off in every direction...after we camped some time, we saw persons riding around over the hills watching us. I was going to the creek to get a bucket of water and found a piece of paper with some writing on it, which read as follows:

"'Captain Kennedy sir, if you should camp here be on your guard for last night we camped here and our stock stampeded and early this morning we went in pursuit of our stock and when about five miles from camp, we found our stock and the Indians driving them off. We had a fight with them. One of our men was killed and two wounded, however we got the stock'. Dated July 18th.

"So double guards were put out and pickets stationed all around but we were not troubled. Everything went off well. Traveled 20 miles today." The Kennedy train that night was camping a few miles west of what is now Big Piney, Wyoming.

McClung's diary continues on July 23, 1862. "After traveling several miles we passed a company of emigrants that had their stock stampeded last night. No doubt the Mormons done it. They were guarding it in their corral when it broke loose, running over tents, wagons and everything which came in their way and broke several wagons in running over them and crippling several of the guards." McClung's comments about Mormon guerillas and his certainty that the Mormons caused a stampede are the first but not the last indications that the emigrants of 1862 were quick to look to the Mormons as the cause for any misfortune.

While McClung's account on July 23 gives the impression that the sky is falling and blames everything on the Mormons, Scott reports the same events dispassionately and never mentions the Mormons as possible perpetrators. "Several trains camped here. They had their stock stampeded, but have them about gathered up now. One train had their cattle corralled and they ran over three wagons and broke them down, slightly wounding two men...Put out picket guards tonight."

Three days later on July 26, when Jane Gould's train reached the same area, she noted that "We hear great stories about the Indians here again...found we had stayed all night on the ground where the Indians had taken some horses from some emigrants who, in trying to recover them, one man lost his life and two others were severely wounded." In spite of "Indian stories" Jane Gould continued, "the children, Arnie and I went strawberrying. Got enough to put in cream for breakfast."

The Dog Law

Hamilton Scott found little to write about on July 24. "Stayed in camp on account of sickness in the company." Then on July 25, "Our cattle stampeded twice last night. We found them all by ten o'clock this morning." McClung had much more to tell us.

"We remained in camp for a day. Several other teams were encamped near us. We enjoyed ourselves finely, but did not know what minute we might be attacked by Indians as there was a train of 105 wagons attacked here last week, three nights in succession. The night passed off fine. Our cattle was brought up at night and guarded as usual, on the outside of the corral and horses staked on the inside. About 11 o'clock our stock stampeded and of all the fuss I ever heard in my life is nothing compared with this. The cattle snorted and ran in every direction, made the mountains fairly quake.

"Every man was up and out in less than no time, but not an Indian was to be seen. We managed to get back the principle part of the cattle tonight and about two o'clock they took another stampede, when two Indians were seen by the guard."

The next day, July 25, McClung continues. "We raised early and started in pursuit of the stock.

There was only a few to be seen. Two companies of us started, one company taking a northeast course and the company I was with the one that took down the creek in the other direction...we found quite a number of good wagons corralled here in those willows and pieces of trunks and harnesses that had been cut to pieces. From the looks, there was no doubt there was a train captured here by the Indians, but would rather think it was those Mormons.

"We returned to camp about noon without seeing or hearing tell of the cattle. However, the other company soon returned with the cattle bringing in pieces of clothing and harnesses, which was found by some wigwam. Everything goes to prove that a small train was captured near this place.

"After the cattle were all gathered together and we were in the act of starting, the cattle took another scare. No one can tell what at. They started to run. Some supposed they were scared by the dogs and, [felt] they might scare them again, so Captain Kennedy called a meeting of the company and passed a dog law. Every dog was to be killed in 30 minutes. This caused a good deal of hard feeling toward Captain Kennedy and several left the train on account of it, but the law was put in force and executed."

Here, McClung sides with Kennedy. "I will just say that Captain Kennedy had a very promising puppy he had bought on the road and had taken a great deal of pains with it. He was ordered to kill it and, having sanctioned the law, he could not refuse, so he took the puppy out of his box and executed him."

Kennedy's position on the "dog law" flap isn't clear from McClung's account. Kennedy called the meeting and the "law" was passed and executed, but Kennedy was "ordered to kill his own puppy", per McClung. Who could order Kennedy to kill his puppy? Perhaps there was a strong anti-dog faction that forced his hand to call the meeting and kill all the dogs. In any case, the issue was a serious one that caused yet another faction, this time the dog owners, to leave the train.

Also, from this incident, you can glimpse democracy in action in its purest form within the wagon train. Kennedy's strategy in calling a meeting at the beginning of the trip to vote for all the officers, the constitution and the by-laws must have established in the minds of all the members of the company that Kennedy's train operated by majority rule and persuaded them that the majority that had approved the "laws" (as Kennedy had designated them), could change or add to those "laws". Certainly Kennedy didn't want to kill his puppy and perhaps Kennedy did not believe a barking dog had been the cause of that very costly stampede. But Kennedy himself had established democracy in the train from the start and, perhaps, he was now 'hoist on his own petard'.

While Scott doesn't mention the dog law or the people who left the train because of it, we do have one other account of the affair. Ellen Paul Garlington, wrote about her memory of the incident many years later. Telling of the stampede, she says, "It took three days to round up enough cattle to start on, the others never being found. Those were three days of terror, for we lived in fear of an Indian attack every minute. Before starting on again, the captain ordered every dog killed. Of course, all hated to give up the dogs, especially the children mourned at losing their pets and it seemed worse out in such a lonesome country. The McGuires had a fine brindle bulldog and how we hated to lose him, since he had watched our tent so faithfully every night."

It's easy to see how the dog issue caused such contention and why some of the emigrants simply couldn't bring themselves to kill their pets. After leaving Independence Rock, the Kennedy train totaled 80 wagons. McClung reported 15 "seceders" departed after the wagon-boat crossing of the river. Five days later, when Jane Gould's train caught up with and passed the Kennedy train, she reported only 36 wagons. Perhaps there were other departures from the company, not mentioned in the diaries. In any case, the "dog law" seems to have prompted a sizeable number to leave the Kennedy train.

After all the dogs were killed, the company moved on up perhaps the most difficult stretch of the trail, up the canyon of what is now shown on maps as South Piney Creek west of Big Piney, Wyoming, along what is now Highway #350. The roadbed on this section of the Landers Cutoff seems to have been largely washed away by the unusually high water that year. McClung, after explaining the dog law incident, continues:

"So we then moved forward from this unfortunate camp crossing deep creeks which were all bank full. H. Creamer upset [his] wagon in the middle of one of these creeks where the water and mud was almost waist deep and cold enough to freeze a man to death. However, we came out all right without damaging the load much this afternoon. There was several wagons broke. We only traveled 10 miles and camped on the Bear River Mountains." Driving up that canyon now on Wyoming Highway #350 brings a question to mind. Why would anyone think building a wagon road there was a good idea?

While McClung, Scott and Jane Gould all refer generally to the mountains of Western Wyoming and Eastern Idaho as the Bear River Mountains, they are now known by several other names, depending on the locality. The mountains in the locality of South Piney Creek are now called the Salt River Range.

It would have been interesting to get Kennedy's view of the stampedes, the "dog law" and the majority vote that required him to kill his own pup.

Since he had a dog himself and had permitted dogs in the train from the beginning, he must have been a dog lover and must have felt a stinging rebuke that the company had voted him down. He certainly was not being accorded the deference envisioned by Captain Crawford, when he advised that the wagon master's decision should be final, "whether right or wrong". Perhaps by this time Kennedy may have been questioning the wisdom the democracy he'd established for the train.

They Seem to be Very Unfortunate

McClung's diary of the following day July 26 tells of more problems. "The road passing over the Bear River Mountains [goes] through some as pretty pine timber as ever lay out of doors. I believe in places the snow was two feet deep. It is going off very fast, which keeps these streams so full. After traveling 15 miles we camped at the foot of the mountain on one fork of Bear River. Grass poor and about eleven o'clock at night, our cattle stampeded again. This caused another great excitement, women and children squalling worse than ten thousand Indians and the cattle making the pine trees fairly crack..."

Hamilton Scott reports the events of July 27. "We remained in camp all day. Thomas Paul's wife died about nine o'clock this morning. She died in childbirth. She has left an infant. She had been very poorly for some time. We buried her this evening under a large pine tree and put a post and paling fence around her grave. Our cattle stampeded last night about eleven o'clock. One hundred and fifty got away. We found them, all but fifteen near."

While the E. E. Ellis family decision to join the wagon train in the sixth month of pregnancy worked out, Thomas Paul's similar decision did not. We don't know other particulars of his wife's death, but certainly her condition must have been aggravated by the extremely difficult travel, her childbirth coming at the worst time of the trip. We do know she had some medical care available to her. In 1942, Martha McGuire Fitzsimmons described the medical care provided in the Kennedy train.

"In our party was a Dr. Collins. He was called on frequently for various ailments and to care for the arrival of new babies, but Captain Kennedy's wife was the midwife and attended to her duties when the occasion demanded, while the wagons went rumbling along." It is hard to believe these 1862 pioneers could think of childbirth and wagons "rumbling along" in the same sentence, but these hardy pioneers accepted such dangers as a normal part of life and childbirth along the trail seems to have been very common, and none of the people who wrote about her death questioned the wisdom of her being on the trip.

James McClung tells us more about Elizabeth Paul's burial and records the poem of remembrance left at the grave-side. "Elizabeth, wife of Thomas Paul died and was buried this afternoon near the foot of the mountain, age 32 years, seven months and 27 days. This is a day of sorrow indeed." Then he records a poem, written for the occasion and perhaps left at the grave-site. He doesn't say who wrote the poem. Perhaps he wrote it himself. The original spelling has been maintained.

"'Friends and physicians could not save this mortal lovely boddy from the grave, nor can the grave confine it here when God commands it to appear. For tho it was her lot to die hear among the mountains high, yet when Gabriel's trump shall sound, among the blessed she will be found, and while she rests beneath this tree, may holy angels watch and see that naught disturbs her peaceful clay, until the dawning of that day."

Elizabeth Paul's grave can still be seen along highway #350, beside a little traveled gravel road about 30 miles west of Big Piney, Wyoming. Nearby are a number of other grave markers of others who died on that trail.

Since leaving Independence Rock, more than three weeks earlier, Jane Gould's wagon train (referred to as the Wilson train) had continued to stay almost exactly three days behind the Kennedy train. By July 28, the day after the death of Elizabeth Paul, Jane Gould's train had made up the three days and caught up with and passed the Kennedy train. The Kennedy train delays due to the stampedes, the dog laws and Elizabeth Paul's death had lengthened their trip by more than three days.

Jane Gould's train faced the same serious difficulty coming up the canyon crossing and re-crossing the flooding creek, but her train kept together, had no stampedes, and did not miss any travel time. Gould describes going up that same canyon. "...(Started) up a canyon following up a creek which we crossed twelve times in ten miles...several [times] the water came into the wagon box. The roads were the worst I ever saw, the creek is unusually high and the road is mostly muddy...the road is washed away in many places...there is one place where the road goes for over a mile over rocks from two inches to two feet large with no gravel or soil between."

The following day, July 28, they had finally caught up with the Kennedy train and her entry that day gives us a dismal picture indeed of the struggling and sad Kennedy train. "Came past a camp of thirty six wagons who have been camped for some time here in the mountains. They have had their cattle stampeded four or five times. There was a woman died in their train yesterday. She left six children and one of them only two days old, poor little thing, it had better have died with its mother. They made a good picket fence around the grave. This same train had a man accidentally shot down at Independence Rock. They seem to be very unfortunate. It is the Kennedy train." The Kennedy train seems to have acquired quite a reputation.

The infant born to Elizabeth Paul lived only a week after her death. Thomas Paul took his remaining six children – not just five as counted by Jane Gould - on to Walla Walla, where he married another member of his own wagon train party, a widow, Susan Ellis Zaring, who already had two children of her own. They settled in Walla Walla where Thomas Paul died in 1904.

Falling Out Again

After burying Elizabeth Paul's body in the morning of July 28, the Kennedy train moved on again in the afternoon. After traveling seven miles, James McClung tells us "we passed a grave by the side of the road and a bloody shirt lying near it with two bullet holes through it and a note written on the head-board reads as follows: 'Opened by Caviness train on the 19th of July. The body was too much decayed to remove.' He was shot with one ball through the temple and one arrow was found by the grave, bloody. The deceased was supposed to be 50 years old. The body [was] not more than six inches underground. Supposed to have been killed by Indians."

James McClung, writing about this murder, as in some other incidents he recorded in his diary, seemed to see himself as a journalist, attempting to learn and record everything he can about the event, even though the murdered man was not connected to the Kennedy train. He conducted an interview with a man "who knew all about the circumstances" and recorded the facts as they were told to him.

"His name was Camel. He was from Pikes Peak with four other wagons. [They] were some three miles behind their train when some 40 Indians came up and were very friendly and wanted to trade horses. They got him off his guard and shot him and wounded several others, but they got away leaving their wagons, teams, clothing and everything behind. The Indians carried off all they could, and burnt the wagons. They took $9000 from Camel."

The figure $9000 is surprising. It is a lot of money now and certainly, much, much more then. If what was told McClung was not an exaggeration, the obvious questions are, first, whether one of these emigrants heading west would ever have had that much money and if he did, why was he carrying so much cash in dangerous country?

$9000 is, in fact a believable figure. One source explains that the cost of traveling to the west and setting up a farm or ranch was very costly, ranging from $2000 to $9000, pointing out that land costs were $1.25 to $10.00 an acre, plus cost of up to $20.00 an acre to clear and break the land. Other costs were draft animals $150 to $200 and a small herd of cattle $500, not to mention outfitting for the trip and maintenance of a family in the new location for a year or so until the new farm or ranch became profitable.

Families moving west, intending to establish a farm or ranch needed a lot of cash. Yet there seems to have been no practical way to send the money ahead safely. They had to take it with them. Within a few more days Kennedy and the Kennedy train were to be confronted with another instance where a large sum of money, $6000 in that case, was stolen in an attack by Indians. It is likely hostile Indians were well aware that many of the emigrants were carrying large sums of money and that was the incentive for some of the attacks.

Jane Gould's train passed the same grave and told much the same story as McClung, with less detail and with no mention of the stolen cash. She saw "an arrow with blood on the point lying by the grave." She also mentions "another new grave a little way from that back in the woods..." Her conclusion: "This is the place of all places for doing foul deeds, with its deep ravines and gorges and thick forests." However, amid this evidence of savage violence, Jane Gould seamlessly transitions to the beauty of the area, continuing: "We found some beautiful flowers in among the mountains, among others is a beautiful white honeysuckle, very much like those we raise in our gardens, only larger."

The next day she and Gus were out picking yellow currants, which she declared "very good when stewed." Jane Gould was not about to permit the fear of Indian attack to spoil those precious little pleasures she was getting from the trip.

Hamilton Scott's diary entry of July 28, didn't mention the grave of the man killed by Indians, but does give us a hint of how seriously the Kennedy train was now taking the problem of their inability to control their stock. Numerous stampedes had taken a heavy toll on the company. "We hitched up at noon and drove ten miles, camping in the timber. No grass for stock. We have our cattle under yoke and chain them to trees."

On July 29 McClung reports the return of some of the cattle lost after the stampede, but also writes about the difficulty they were having controlling their oxen motive power. "Last night the boys came up with four head of cattle which they found some ten miles from camp leaving eleven head supposed to be driven off by the Indians, the cattle having had nothing to eat for one day and night, they were very hard to drive. Having been scared almost to death, makes them a great deal harder to manage. In crossing a small ravine in making a turn on the opposite side, I got (almost?) too near the bank and the wagon tumbled over in the ravine, falling some 20 feet. As it fell, the coupling came loose. The hind wheels and the bed went to the bottom leaving the front wheels to the cattle. It mashed the bows all to pieces and breaking one chair. Nothing else hurt. We were right very soon and traveling on."

On July 30, McClung reported: "The company falling out with Kennedy. There was another division. We traveled on leaving six or eight wagons behind. Some ten miles [we] camped on good grass and before long those we left behind came in sight of us and camped near us." If there were only 36 wagons on July 28, as counted by Jane Gould, the Kennedy train, with the new losses, had now become a small company. There is no hint here of what issue caused the new rift and Hamilton Scott never even mentioned it. By writing that the falling out was "with Kennedy", McClung implies another disagreement with Kennedy personally, rather than some other reason.

The next day McClung writes that "in eight miles of here we came to Salt Creek. Here we could have gathered bushels of as pure and white salt as I ever have seen anywhere. After traveling 12 miles, we camped on a creek in the edge of the timber and presently, the other company came up and corralled with us, all but one man by the name of R. Cummins, our Justice of the Peace. He passed by and we never seen him any more, but he caught up with the Culberson's train."

James McClung's diary entry confirms that Robert Cummins, one of the original elected officers of the Kennedy company finally joined some of the earlier defectors in a train headed by Ed Culberson, another of the original officers. Culberson and Cummins must have been close associates of Kennedy in Iowa and Kennedy himself must have picked both of them as officers of the train. Some forty years later, Robert Cummins wrote a short summary of some of the events of his trip with the Kennedy train, noting he had been elected "judge" for the train. He never mentioned in his account that he had finished the journey with another train, nor was that information passed down to his descendants.

However, Robert Cummins' son Woodson Cummins, age seven at the time of the trip, confirmed at least part of the story of the split with the Kennedy train. In his later years, in the 1930s, Woodson enjoyed telling stories about his wagon train trip to his grandchildren. While the adults may not have been interested in his stories, or were too busy to listen, the grandchildren listened with rapt attention. How much of what he related came from his own recollections and how much from what he was told by his parents, isn't clear. The most memorable of his stories told us of watching the firing squad execute the man found guilty of murder.

Woodson Cummins also told of the split with the main train. "We'd been on the trail for a long time and the progress was very slow. We were behind schedule. So my father and several other men from the wagon train decided to go on ahead by themselves. That afternoon we camped on top of a little hill. Everything was fine until it got dark. Then we looked around us and saw Indian campfires on the hills around us.

"All the men armed themselves and stationed themselves around those few wagons, ready for an Indian attack at any moment. All the rest of us stayed close together in the wagons. I've never been so scared in all by life. We were sure the Indians were going to attack and we'd all be killed. Nobody slept at all that night. But when morning came we were still alive. The Indians had not attacked and, as fast as we could, we drove the wagons back to the main wagon train." While Woodson's story may have strayed a bit from what actually happened, it seems to have confirmed the same incident.

Judgment on Him and His Train

The Kennedy train had endured some serious disasters, deaths and difficulty with stampedes. But back on the road again, things seemingly in control, James McClung's morale appears to have brightened as he pens his diary entry of August 1, 1862. He seems to be writing for an audience. "...I gazed for a moment and said within myself, as I glanced over the beautiful valleys surrounded by the mountains, how beautiful are the works of nature, the beautiful pine trees with their heads towering above the lofty mountains and the silver streams winding their way from the top to the bottom."

McClung continues on an up-beat mood on August 3rd. "...we have passed over the Rattlesnake Mountains, the Rocky Mountains and the Bear River Mountains, and a fine level road [is] before us." (The wagon train had crossed the border from Wyoming into what is now Idaho, near the Wyoming towns of Auburn and Fairview.) Then McClung describes another very serious stampede.

"We was in fine spirits and traveling with speed when some loose horses from another train come running up behind us and scared the hind teams in our train. They started and run and from this, the whole train took a general stampede, the wagons running in every direction, some of them upsetting and scattering the load and breaking several wagons. However, this was nothing as a wagon run over Mrs. Nancy Townson, wife of Mr. Townson, who died from the wound at twelve o'clock, leaving one child three years old and several others was severely hurt."

Hamilton Scott's diary entries for the time were similar. On August 2nd, "Between eleven and twelve o'clock, our cattle [were] scared at some loose horses belonging to another train. About 25 teams ran away, upsetting and breaking wagons, running over men, women and children. Mrs. Townsend from Monroe, Iowa was dangerously wounded. Wilson Scott had a broken leg. Mrs. Hoover's head was bruised."

Scott continues the following day, "Thomas Paul's child died last night and Mrs. Townsend, who was so seriously hurt in the stampede, died about twelve o'clock today. We buried them this evening. The others are all getting better." Wilson Scott, whose leg was broken in the stampede was Hamilton Scott's brother.

Hamilton Scott's other brother, Robert C. Scott wrote the most colorful and complete account of the stampede that took the life of Mrs. Townsend. Robert Scott's account, in the form of a diary, seems to have been written sometime after the trip as an elaboration on Hamilton Scott's diary. Robert's entry for August 2 follows.

"About 11 o'clock a loose horse run up by some ox teams. The cattle have had the jitters more than we. Scare at anything. We think they smell the Indians. The horse scared the cattle as he ran by them. The cattle give a big snort and away they went, tails up. About 25 teams ran away, upset wagons, ran over men, women and children and jumped over each other and scattered everything over the rocky roads and over high banks. Hurt a lot of people, some very seriously. It was a terrible mix-up.

"Mrs. Townsend of Monroe, Iowa, died later in the afternoon from being run over. Wilson Scott from Fremont had a leg broken. Mr. Hoover had body injuries and 32 others bruised, sprained and scratched. Wagons badly broken, etc. It was the worst mess ever. I can't describe it. We had to travel a while with only two oxen on a wagon to be able to handle them, they are so badly scared. The cattle we loosened from the wagons were still in the yokes and chained together. They would hist their tails and snort every 20 or 30 minutes and try to get away. We had to keep them away from those hitched to the wagons to keep them from running away again. We only traveled 8 miles after the runaway, and camped the first place we found where we could stop and let the cattle get quiet down over night."

McClung, using a different spelling, also tells of Nancy Townsend's death and burial. "At twelve o'clock Mrs. Townson died, and at three o'clock, she was buried, age 21 years. The day was spent in repairing wagons and fixing to travel."

Sometime after Jane Gould's train had caught and passed the Kennedy train on July 28, Kennedy regained the lead. Then, on August 3, 1862, delayed by the stampede, deaths and burials, Kennedy was again passed by Jane Gould's train. Her diary entry for that day enumerates the various reverses suffered by the Kennedy train and provides an explanation which nineteenth century Americans would have found highly plausible: the judgment of God.

"We passed by [the Kennedy train]. They had just buried the babe of the woman who died a few days ago, and were just digging a grave for another woman that was run over by the cattle and wagons when they stampeded yesterday. She lived twenty-four hours. She gave birth to a child a short time before she died. The child was buried with her. She leaves a little two year old girl and a husband. They say he is nearly crazy with sorrow.

"The captain of this Canady or Kennedy train is the man who arrested Young (that murdered Scott) and ordered him to be shot. He did not belong to this train, but to another. Some say that it is a judgment upon him and his train for meddling with and depriving a man of his life without the aid of the law. After cattle have been frightened once or twice, there is no safety with them. Yesterday there were several loose horses came running up when the whole train of cattle started pell-mell, crippled two men besides killing the woman. They mark nearly half their camps with dead cattle. I never supposed that cattle would run so in the yoke and hitched to the wagon."

Here would have been a good time to interview Jane Gould. She could have answered a number of questions. Certainly it would have been interesting to ask her how she was enjoying the trip. Her journal neatly balances reports about her enjoyment of berry picking, scenery and the flowers she discovers with reports of murders and stampedes. She certainly seems to be a person who would find pleasure in varied circumstances. Also, it would be interesting to question her about her own attitude about the execution of Young. Is she just reporting what some in her train think or does she herself think God is punishing the Kennedy train?

In reporting on the repeated stampedes in the Kennedy train, it would be interesting to get her view of why her train was better able to control their oxen.

On to the Snake River

The Kennedy train had had nothing but trouble with their cattle. Time after time stampedes had wreaked havoc in the form of injuries and damage to their precious, irreplaceable wagons and equipment, and now a death. Starting again on August 4th, they tried something different, according to McClung. "We again traveled on, dividing the train into four parts and traveling one-fourth mile apart, to avoid more trouble. I taking the lead, rode on....During the day, we passed several nice streams and, traveling 25 miles, we camped."

Hamilton Scott records the change too. "Our cattle being so unsafe to travel all together, we divided the company in four parts and traveled some distance apart, all camping together at night. Drove 20 miles and camped on a branch of Snake River." Then on August 5th, "Drove twenty miles, camped on Snake River." The new system seemed to work.

On August 5, both James McClung and Jane Gould reported the end of the Landers Cutoff and rejoining the main overland trail to Oregon and California. Jane Gould, lamenting the dust on the trail cried out in her diary: "if I could just have a hot bath... Camped on a rise of ground where the Salt Lake and Fort Hall comes in." Her reference was to where the Landers Cutoff rejoined the main trail, a few miles southeast of Fort Hall, Idaho.

The Kennedy train and Jane Gould's train (the Wilson train) were now close together, for James McClung also reported on August 5th rejoining the main trail. "In the afternoon we struck the old Oregon road, where we passed several trains that was in camp...our travels is 25 today." On August 6th, McClung reported "the roads is so dusty at times we can hardly see our teams...About 10 o'clock we passed opposite Fort Hall which is some six miles from the road on our right. The Fort is vacated...some Frenchman, that had squaws for wives had a traveling post; sold flour at 12 dollars per hundred."

When McClung started his diary, he told us his destination was the Salmon River mines. On August 6th he notes they had reached the road that led to the Salmon River mines which "was only 200 miles and a good level road; and told us that hundreds had gone that road. They also said that the mines was very rich and extensive. But none of us went that road and it was very well.

"We afterward learned several companies had tried it and gone as far as they could with their wagons [then] packed their teams with provisions, leaving their wagons and many other things behind; which those Mormons and Frenchman got and took to Salt Lake and sold. Those companies found it impassible, turned back and packed through to Oregon."

McClung never explains why he changed his mind about going to the Salmon River mines, but his diary sounds a sigh of relief that he didn't follow through on his original plan.

On August 7th Scott writes "Eleven miles brought us to a branch of Snake River which we had to ferry, costing us one dollar and fifty cents per wagon. Drove one mile more and camped, making twelve miles. I gathered some very nice currants this evening. We will have some pies. We are now opposite Fort Hall, eight miles distance."

While Scott reports on the ferry without editorial comment, McClung is indignant at what he views as a rip-off by the Mormons. "Here was some Mormons that had a ferry. They had taken the government bridge away and built a dam, some 75 yards below the ferry...and dammed the water up and charged one dollar and a half a wagon to ferry us across and we swam our stock."

Again behind the Kennedy train, Jane Gould reached the $1.50 ferry the following day, August 8. "...we ferried on two large skiffs fastened together and poles laid across, took two wagons at a time, paid a dollar and a half apiece. Here we saw some Shoshone or Snake Indians. There were four or five Mormon wagons here trading. They sold flour to some of the trains for ten dollars per hundred. Charley bought a dozen onions; traded some caps for them. They sell them for two cents apiece. They are brought from Salt Lake. We had an onion soup for supper, which was very good." While McClung was indignant at what he saw as highway robbery, Jane Gould paints a different picture: "The ferrymen were quite gentlemanly fellows for this part of the world."

None of the three diarists say it, but they must have been feeling some relief, having made it through the lonesome and difficult mountain country. It was now much warmer. The roads were now more nearly level. Now, on the main overland road, they were seeing much more wagon train traffic and more people after the joining of the two routes of the trail, leading to a feeling of safety in numbers.

There were even people up from Salt Lake City with produce to sell them and ferrymen, ready to take their boats across streams, for a price. Even though, to McClung, they were the hated Mormons, or Frenchmen with squaw wives, they must have helped lift a little of the fear of Indian attacks that had colored everything these emigrants had done and thought about on the trip west. While there were still no United States cavalry forces anywhere near the emigrant trains, surely, if they had escaped Indian attack up in the lonely mountains, the Indians wouldn't attack them now that they were traveling in such numbers along the Snake River.

Two days after the Kennedy train had crossed the Snake tributary, both McClung and Scott describe their view of American Falls on the Snake River. McClung on August 9 says "...we struck the Snake River. Here the stream is 50 yards wide, very swift, deep and clear. After traveling one mile down the river, we came to the American Falls and here I again must remark was another curiosity to see the bright water of the Snake River falling almost 70 feet, where you can hear it roaring for miles."

Scott reports on the falls too, in more sparing language and with a more accurate estimate of the height of the falls. "This is one of the natural curiosities. The water falls forty or fifty feet over rocks and makes a great roaring noise." However, none of the emigrants would have time to look at the natural curiosities for awhile. The very presence of such a large number of emigrants and white traders, seemingly taking over their lands, had infuriated the Shoshones and Chief Pocatello was preparing a reception for some of them.

A Perfect State of Frenzy

Writing in 1937, an anonymous writer employed in the Federal Writers Project, did as good a job as any of the wagon train survivors describing the wagon trains as they made their way slowly along the Oregon-California Trail in Southeastern Idaho through Chief Pocatello's territory. "...Behind [the driver of the first wagon] in the crawling wagons, reaching back for a quarter of a mile, were men and women sitting in stupor, with tired flesh and tired eyes; solemn children who had sat in these loaded wagons week after week, going they hardly knew where...

"This was a hot day in August with not a tree in sight and with no breeze. The yellow earth was turned up by the wheels in lazy blinding clouds that rolled back from wagon to wagon and settled upon the freight until the travelers could write their names in dust an inch deep...it was not until the leader had passed into the small gorge, with refreshing shadow on either side, that a sudden movement in the stones above brought every man to a trigger...The sudden confusion and panic, the awful horror of the next few minutes is almost impossible to realize."

Bert Webber in his book, Oregon Trail, Emigrant Massacre of 1862 gives us some background on the mood of Chief Pocatello and the Shoshone Indians in

1862. "Indians in southern Idaho had been nervous about the encroachment of the whites onto their land for some time...Small groups, often on their own away from large trains could expect trouble most anywhere in southeastern Idaho...Pocatello, who became conspicuous as a Shoshone leader before 1860, decided that the pioneers and their wagons could no longer cross his territory. This area extended from American Falls past the Raft River..."

All who survived the Indian attack remembered and told or wrote about it. While the details differ in all of the accounts, looking at a number of them gives us a pretty good idea what happened. Sarah Zaring Howard's account, decades later, tells us: "One day when we were traveling along at our usual gait and had rather become used to dangers we were in, we suddenly came in sight of eight wagons out a little way from the road. The wagons were stripped of everything and there were no teams in sight.

"When our train came nearer, two or three survivors of that train came to us and told their story, how the Indians had surprised them and came up while they were at their noon lunch...Well, our people stopped and helped those people to find and bury their dead and gather up what they could find of the stock and a few articles of clothing which the Indians dropped in their hurry."

Hamilton Scott's diary of August 9 tells how the Kennedy train became aware of the attack. "When we stopped for dinner, there was a man came riding back and told us the Indians were robbing a train about four miles ahead and they wanted assistance. Some of the men started immediately, the rest hitching up without finishing our dinner and drove on as fast as we could punch our teams along but before we got there, the Indians had driven the emigrants away and had taken all their stock and provisions, clothing and everything.

"They had gone, leaving the empty and naked wagons, even taking the covers off the wagons. It was only a small train of eleven teams. There were not less than two hundred Indians that made the attack. There were only twenty-five men in the train and a few women. They killed one man and wounded another in the arm and seriously wounded one woman who was shot in the neck. We took them in and hauled their wagons to a suitable camping place about four miles away. We will make arrangements to take them along with us. Here we found a horse train of about twelve wagons that was attacked about the same time that the other train was. Eight of their horses were stolen and two of their men killed."

Hamilton Scott's brother Robert described the event in an account probably written sometime later. "While we were eating dinner, a man on a horse rushed up to us and called out in excitement, 'The Indians are robbing a train 4 miles ahead.

Come quick.' About 145 men grabbed their guns, mounted horses and rushed over there as fast as the horses could go, leaving men to care for our own train to come on. We met a number of the emigrants coming to meet us, crying for help, big strong men and women, stood there crying like children. They had to run for their lives, were bareheaded, barefooted, with nothing left but what was on their backs, had to run and let the Indians take everything but the wagons. They got into some timber in the foothills out of sight. We followed them a long way until about 4 o'clock.

"They knew we were after them so they scattered in the hills and timber. We only got 14 oxen. They could not travel so fast and our men run up on them, and the Indians ran. They took all provisions, bedding and stock, all but the wagons and yokes and chains, emptied out feather and straw beds. This was a small train, only 18 wagons and 25 men, so they had no chance against about 200 Indians. They were attacked in a narrow canyon, where there were lots of big rocks to hide behind, big as a house. The Indians never come out in the open or put up a square fight. They always sneak and hide behind rocks or trees. Even behind their horses and shoot, from hideouts. They crawl among trees and rocks like snakes or rats.

"We got the cattle back to where the wagons were, and our own train had come up and was waiting for us. The Indians only killed one man, Mr. Bullwinkel from New York, but wounded several men and one woman. We took these people in with us, tied their wagons behind ours and hauled them 4 or 5 miles and camped.

'We will divide up so they can get along and take them on through, give women and men clothing and food and put oxen on their wagons to get along. We could do nothing less and be human. And they were very thankful for help. All the people of the west will help each other when in trouble. This was a bad spot for people to be in, robbed of everything, nothing to eat or wear or a way to travel and out in this wild Indian west with nothing at all, and no way to get anything. It was a miracle we came along.

"When we went into camp there were 12 wagons in another train came to us and asked to stay with our train until we all got through. They had been attacked today at another place and lost 8 horses and two men were killed by Indians. They had a hard fight, but saved most of their outfit, but were badly scared and did not want to travel alone anymore."

James McClung's diary of August 9 tells more: "We stopped to take dinner on the bank of a little brook when two men came running up on horseback and said their train, which was some three miles ahead, was attacked by an overwhelming number of Indians and our assistance was needed forthwith. We accordingly moved forward. Before arriving at the scene of the action, we met a woman that had been shot through the breast and also a number of children which were in a perfect state of frenzy. The woman died in a few days.

"When we arrived at the scene of action, we found one dead man, several wounded, five in number. Their stock had all been stolen together with all their provisions. The man killed was Bullwinkle from New York City. He was robbed of between 6 and 7 thousand dollars. All the effects of the party were taken, even to their beds and clothing. We took care of the unfortunate train. Before leaving the unfortunate camp, we found two wagons which had been upset and partly robbed. Here we found a dead man lying nearby. We brought him along. We traveled a half mile farther and overtook another train that had camped. The Indians had attacked them and had killed the man we picked up and one more and wounded three. Here we camped for the night to bury the dead."

Jane Gould in the Wilson train, now a day behind Kennedy, arrived on the scene of the attack on the following day. Her diary entry of that day, August 10, 1862 tells a story with more details than either of the Scotts or McClung. "...we from the back end of the train saw those on ahead all get out their guns. In a short time the word came back that a train six miles on had been attacked by the Indians and some killed and that was cause enough for the arming. In a short time, we were met by two men. They wanted us to go a short distance from the road and bring up two dead men to this camp five miles ahead. Albert unloaded his little wagon and sent Gus back with them and about forty armed men from both trains to get them.

"We learned that a train of eleven wagons had been plundered of all that was in them and the teams taken and three men killed. One was Mr. Bullwinkle, who left us the 25th of last month at the crossing of the Green River. He went with this Adams train, was intending to wait for us, but we had not overtaken him yet. He was shot eight times and his dog was shot four times before he would let them get to the wagon. They took all that he had in his wagon except his trunks and books and papers. They broke open his trunks and took all that they contained (he had six). It is supposed that they took six thousand dollars from him. [They] tore the cover from his wagon. It was oil cloth. He had four choice horses. They ran away when he was shot...The Captain (Adams) had a daughter shot and wounded severely. This happened yesterday."

My God John!

Mr. John C. Hillman, who had been a member of the Kennedy train earlier in the trip, but had later joined another train, gave perhaps the most complete account of the attack in a letter home, written on August 11, describing the attack on August 9.

"...we were in the very midst of danger and seemed to be almost entirely unconscious of it....I saw a horseman coming towards me in a hasty manner... On his approaching me, I discovered it was a man belonging to our wagon...The first thing he said to me was 'My God, John, the Indians have massacred a train and robbed them of all they had and they are only a short distance from us.'...In an hours driving, we came to the place where the horrible scene took place, but found the Indians had run off the stock, taking the provisions, clothing etc. of the train, but left the wagons, which the ox trains ahead of us had taken and gone on in pursuit of grass.

"The place selected for the attack was the best on the road and not far distant from the road which turns down to Salt Lake....Here we pushed on, endeavoring to overtake them, but only got a short distance on account of the darkness and were obliged to camp on the very ground where the Indians had, a few hours previous, made ring

123

with their pandemonium shouts, and red with the blood of innocent men and women....

"We pushed on at daybreak for the ox teams and grass, which we found in a camp five miles distant. I found three men killed and several wounded. One woman mortally wounded and the wagons which the Indians had left. Two of the men killed were from Iowa City, A. H. Winter and an Italian whose name I did not learn. The other man was from New York City. Bullwinkle was his name and it is said he had some $6000 which was taken from him."

Since she was only five years old at the time of the attack, we would hesitate to give great credit to the memories Christena Taylor Chambers had of the attack 87 years later. She was 92 when she was quoted in a Portland Oregonian news story. However, her father, Ephraim Taylor was severely wounded in the fight Kennedy had with the Indians the following day. We can assume her father and mother reinforced whatever memory she had of the attack. No doubt, what she saw as a small child and the memory of her father's serious injury stayed with her throughout her life.

Her account sounds as reliable as the accounts of witnesses made at the time. "On August 9 when they needed help, there were no soldiers near. The Indians were well aware of it. Near American Falls on the Snake River a train of 12 or 15 horse-drawn wagons, the 'New Yorkers', was ambushed.

One man rode back a few miles to get help from Kennedy's train. A number of armed men hurried to the scene and later the ox train was brought up and encamped....It was the most awful sight, with dead people on the ground, dead and wounded horses, women and children crying, wagons burning; flour, sugar and feathers scattered on the earth where the Indians had ripped sacks, beds and wagon covers to get cloth."

Ellen Paul Garlington, a ten year old member of the Kennedy train, like others who wrote about the attack on the "New Yorkers", included in her later account the assertion that the Adams train, referred to as the "New Yorkers", were wealthy; also, that the Mormons may have had something to do with the attack. "A wealthy outfit with a dozen or more wagons, all horse-drawn and well provisioned from New York, were crossing the plains only for adventure and excitement...Redskins had attacked them and this man had ridden back to us for help.

"Captain Kennedy hurried a number of men ahead, but when they arrived, the Indians had gone, after killing five of the party, taking all the horses, cattle and provisions, even their feather beds and wagon covers...It was said their train had been watched for some days by the reds because they surmised it was a wealthy outfit. Also, it was strongly believed the Mormons were helping the redskins, for during the attack our men were sure they heard voices of whites giving orders to the Indians, and were convinced they were voices of Mormons..."

While Mrs. Garlington's description of the attack itself closely follows other accounts, it reveals what must have been a general distrust and suspicion of the Mormons among the emigrants. While there seems to be no basis for implicating the Mormons in the Idaho attack, the emigrants were probably all aware of the vicious attack on a wagon train in Southeastern Utah, just five years before, in 1857. That attack, referred to as the Mountain Meadows Massacre, on the Fancher-Baker wagon train resulted in the murder of more than 120 people as well as the kidnapping of 17 very young children. Although some of the facts are still in dispute, evidence indicates some Mormon leaders participated in the attack.

Mrs. Garlington's account perhaps also reveals a resentment of the "New Yorkers'" wealth. They had crossed the plains only for "adventure and excitement." They were not worthy farmers on a journey to resettle on new lands. They even had feather beds in their wagons! More than likely the Iowa emigrants' beds were of straw.

A Mr. H. F. Swasley wrote an account of the affair published in the Union, a newspaper in Quincy, Illinois October 28, 1862. Swasley, not a member of the Kennedy train, provides some information not included in other accounts. He cites a smaller number of Indians who participated in the attacks, "seventy-five to one hundred mounted Indians, who commenced a rapid fire from their ponies. Adams formed his wagons as speedily as possible into a corral shape, and his men prepared themselves as well as circumstances would permit to make defense, but to little account, for the Indians would ride in on their ponies to within long range, fire, then retreat to reload...

"Towards evening, several trains came along and the fugitives gathered into camp. Newman and Kennedy's train took up the survivors and that night a corral of eighty-six wagons was formed, while a little later, Thompson's train of twenty wagons came up and camped in the vicinity, which made us feel more safe.

Even the San Francisco Bulletin published an account on September 27, 1862, without attributing a source. While they got some of the information wrong, for example that the attack occurred "on the Landers Cutoff", they did supply some colorful language missing in the other accounts. "...After passing Salmon Falls...Charles Bullwinkle had taken a little liquor and was free in showing his money and nice firearms—one of which he sold to some of the whites or Indians who loaf around the ferry at the Falls...Bullwinkle was shot dead by the identical gun, no doubt, which he had sold...

"They knew that white men were concerned in the massacre, for some 15 were seen lying on a high bench of land beckoning and directing the Indians.

Bullwinkle had $7000 of his own money stolen; Adams had $3000 and others had enough to make the sum of about $20,000, all of which was lost by the pillaged train, exclusive of their stock, wagons, clothing, food, and the valuable lives taken by the fiends in human shape, who appear to infest that part of the route for no other purpose than to murder and rob for a livelihood."

The reporter's account must have provided exciting news to his San Francisco readers.

I Am a Dead Man

John Knox Kennedy's reaction to the Indian attack on the two small wagon trains was perhaps predictable. None of the accounts of what happened the next day, August 10, 1862 make any mention of a discussion as to what to do. All of the accounts, like Hamilton Scott's quoted here, simply start out with what Kennedy did.

"The next morning, Sunday, August 10, Captain Kennedy, with thirty-five armed men, started in pursuit of the Indians to recover the stolen property. When about nine miles from camp, a band of Indians came on their horses, meeting the party. The Indians at once raised a white flag. One of the boys shot at them. The Indians immediately raised a war whoop and began circling our boys. They fought them for about three miles, killing two of our company and wounding several others. Captain Kennedy, mortally wounded, shot through the side just above the hip bone. Tom Newman and one other missing, supposed to be killed. There is now four or five trains camped here."

Hamilton Scott's account above, gives some specific details about Kennedy's battle with the Indians, but it is not a first person account and we can assume Scott was not part of Kennedy's "thirty-five armed men." Moreover, he was incorrect to record Kennedy's wounds as mortal. While a number of survivors have described the August 10 battle, all but one appear to be third person accounts and none of the accounts exactly agree. Only the version written by Robert Scott some time later seems to be an eye-witness account. He was there, one of Kennedy's 35 volunteers, and participated. We are not aware of another first hand account by a participant.

Robert Scott's description of the August 10 action abundantly filled with the words "we" and "us" follows: "Captain Kennedy with 35 men went out to try and get the 8 horses back. Out about 9 miles in the hills, the Indians were guarding the horses in a canyon. When they saw us they began riding around the stolen stock, in a circle and shooting arrows under the horses neck, hanging on the opposite side from us. There were about 75 to 100 Indians. We stood our ground and after we had dropped about 20 Indians they became scattered and in 20 minutes more they all were out in every direction and gone. We surrounded the horses and brought them in to camp.

"We lost two of our men in the fight. Thomas Newman from our train and one man from the other train, don't know his name, were killed by the Indians. These men got away from the rest of us and were killed. Captain Kennedy was shot through the side and Mr. Taylor through the leg, and several others got slight wounds. We had to carry Capt. Kennedy and Taylor on stretchers, because they could not stand the jolt of the wagons. Men took turns carrying."

While Robert Scott's account seems to be the only certain eye witness account, it's possible James McClung was also one of the 35 volunteers Kennedy took with him into battle with the Indians. After all, he was or had been a member of the Independent Braves, and his diary entry includes the kind of details an eye witness would notice. But McClung's account of Kennedy's battle includes no we's or us's; it is the account of an observer or a journalist, not a participant. Perhaps McClung saw himself as a journalist and purposely took himself out of the story as many good journalists do, both in reporting Kennedy's fight with the Indians and in his account of the execution of Young, earlier in the trip.

In McClung's August 10 diary entry, his praise of Kennedy is hard to square with his later negative comments about him. However, after Kennedy's battle with the Indians, Kennedy was, at least temporarily, a sainted hero to McClung. "There was 200 wagons came up last night and camped with us. Captain Kennedy acted the part of a man and proved himself worthy of the gratitude which was exhibited by the emigrants. On the occasion he took the company of Independent Braves and started in pursuit of the stolen stock and when about 7 miles from camp, he was attacked by several hundred Indians on horseback against 30 odd whites.

"Here a desperate fight took place which lasted several hours, when Kennedy had to retreat under a heavy crossfire for 3 miles. He was severely wounded in the side, but, being on horseback, he still fought and gave orders. He lost 4 men killed and 7 wounded. The Indians loss is unknown, but thought to be 15. Among the killed was George Leaper from Marion County, Iowa and George Adams of Marion County, Iowa. The others were left on the field and afterwards could not be found. Those left on the field were William Mouts from Washington County, Iowa and Thomas Newman from Wapello County, Iowa, near Dahlonga.

"He was wounded in the breast in the retreat and no doubt could have been saved if he could have had a horse to have ridden, but, becoming weak and faint from loss of blood and fatigue, he stopped when the Indians were in a few rods of him. One of the boys [looked] back and he said, 'Take care of yourselves for I am a dead man'. The field was searched over and over again. There was nothing left on the field except four dead ponies and pools of blood."

Chief Pocatello Dressed in Bullwinkle's Suit

Jane Gould's diary of August 10 also tells of Kennedy's battle with the Indians. "This morning a part of [the Adams train] and a part of the Kennedy train went in pursuit of the stock. They were surrounded by Indians on ponies, two killed, several wounded and two supposed to be killed. They were never found. One of those killed was Captain Adams' son. The other was a young man in the Kennedy train. Those that were carried to camp were those killed this morning. Mr. Bullwinkle and two others were buried before we got to the camp. There were one hundred and fifty wagons there and thirty-four of ours.

"Captain Kennedy was severely wounded. Captain Hunter of the Iowa City train was killed. Likewise an Italian... We could not get George (Jane Gould's ten year old son) to ride after the news. He would walk and carry his loaded pistol. If there was any shooting going on, he wanted to help."

On the following day, Jane Gould tells of the burials. "The two men that we brought up were buried early this morning with the other three, so they lie five men side by side in this vast wilderness, killed by the guns and arrows of the red demons. The chief appeared yesterday in a suit of Mr. Bullwinkle's. On the battlefield, some of them had the best kind of rifles..."

Only Jane Gould noted that "the chief" appeared the very day of Kennedy's battle with the Indians, dressed in Mr. Bullwinkle's suit. Was the chief Jane Gould saw so finely attired, Chief Pocatello? If the chief did appear in Bullwinkle's fine New York suit, why wasn't he confronted by vigilante justice in the same way murderer Young was confronted, captured and executed by Kennedy earlier in the trip?

Perhaps the answer can be found in the number of hostile Indians, flushed with their victory over the white violators of their territory, close at hand. Moreover, not only was there no civil authority of any kind in the area, but the nearest army contingent was hundreds of miles away. By the time the emigrants of Kennedy's train and the other trains counted and buried their dead, they just wanted to get out with the lives and property that remained.

While Jane Gould wrote no more in her diary about Mr. Bullwinkle, a comment about him had been added by her son, T. T. Tourtillott, on the copy of her diary in my possession, perhaps supplying information his mother had told him. His note reads: "This man Bullwinkle, having plenty of horse flesh and not a very heavy load – no passengers but his large St. Bernard dog - became impatient and, disregarding all advice about Indian hazard, moved on in advance of our group and finally joined the next train. It was said that his trunks contained merchandise to be sold upon his arrival in California."

On August 12, Jane Gould tells of the death of Captain Adams' daughter and tells us that she "was buried in a box made of a wagon box. Poor father and mother lost one son and one daughter, all of his teams, clothing and four thousand dollars [and] is left dependent on the bounty of strangers."

Both Martha McGuire Fitzsimmons and Christena Taylor Chambers, also told something about Kennedy's battle with the Indians. Fitzsimmons remembered only that "some of the men went to try to find and punish the Indians. Some of the men never returned. Captain Kennedy was wounded by a poisoned arrow".

Christina Chamber, whose father Ephraim Taylor was wounded while part of the Kennedy search party adds to the details we have from others. However the number she shows as killed is not verified by any other account. "Kennedy got 25 men and tried to recapture some of the horses. The party was surrounded and fought for hours that day...They might as well have been killed had not another group of emigrants, the 'Missouri Train', come into sight about sundown. The Indians withdrew.

"Seven men were killed and six were wounded, including the captain...A few Indians had guns but most of them fought with bow and arrow and scalping knife. Among those counted dead were two wounded men who had to be abandoned and could not be found later. Undoubtedly, Indians took them away...Among the wounded was Ephraim Taylor, shot through the side and back. The wound was cleansed by drawing a silk handkerchief through it, and he recovered".

Margaret Stoot Thiel, who was sixteen in 1862 also told the story of her step-father's search party and subsequent fight with the Indians. "Father called for volunteers and a number of the men took their guns and started out. Soon they sighted the Indians, but they so outnumbered father's men that he decided to return to protect his own train from a similar attack. "The Indians however, attacked before he could withdraw, killing a Mr. Newman who started west leaving a family of five. Our men never found the body..."

The diary of Henry M. Judson, a member of a wagon train traveling shortly behind the Kennedy train on August 9, 1862, repeats much of the story told by others, including the figure $6000 taken from Bullwinkle. He also covers some ground omitted by others. "Our camp is a sorry one today (August 10), scarcely a smile to be seen and the jokes are infrequent. Capt Kennedy sells at auction the effects of the dead to supply the pressing wants of the poor wretches who have been robbed...an express rider comes from below for the Dr to attend Capt Kennedy who led the volunteers this AM.

"He reports that about 5 miles back from the road they came upon Indians, 20 in number with the stock. The Indians are armed with rifles which carry 200 yds and at the first fire, a part of the volunteers stampede. Capt K in trying to rally them is mortally wounded. They fall back to the road where there is an ox train of 10 or 12 wagons and when our informant left, were trying to keep the Indians at bay."

It's hard to reconcile Judson's estimate of 20 Indians, with other much larger estimates. The "20" figure could be an error in transcribing the original. Since Kennedy's men were outnumbered, there must have been more than 20 Indians. McClung's "several hundred" could be right, but his estimates usually seem to be on the high side, particularly when he refers to Indians. Robert Scott's figure of "75 to 100" may be more credible, but it's doubtful anyone spent much time counting the Indians Kennedy's volunteers were fighting.

Not mentioned in other accounts, reinforcements were then sent to help Kennedy, according to Judson. "Joe and Jack with our guest L. Billman of Iowa joining a party to go to their assistance which is immediately off. Captain Bristol with a few more soon follow making a reinforcement of 30 or 35 men."

Like others, Judson repeats the allegation that Mormons are behind the attacks without noting any basis for such a belief. "It is believed that these depredations are instigated and led by Mormon men with white blood in their veins...All are agreed that they are led by a good proportion of white men, perhaps renegades and perhaps not from Salt Lake. Some think they have recognized men seen at the ferry of the Pont-Newf...

"Six Indians and some ponies are known to be killed. 4 of Capt Kennedy's company are killed and 3 wounded, himself among the latter and tis feared mortally. Two of his men who were killed were left among the Indians from necessity." Then the following day "...An effort is made to start a mounted party of 100 men to recover the bodies of the 2 missing men, but Capt K's advice strongly urged, is taken and the idea is abandoned."

Hamilton Scott's journal for August 11 and 12, covers the aftermath of the battles. "We have buried five men side by side. We think it is not safe to go back to hunt the other two for fear we lose more. Newman was seen to fall in the battle. We hitched up and drove thirteen miles and camped on Raft River. Captain Kennedy very poorly. The loss of property and money was today estimated to be fifteen thousand dollars."

Then on the twelfth, "Miss Adams, the lady who was wounded in the fight with the Indians, died last night and was buried this morning. Some of the trains take the California road this morning. We keep the old Oregon Road. Drove eighteen miles, camped on a creek." (The Wilson train and Jane Gould were now on their way south toward California.)

McClung's diary entries for the same two days cover much the same information. "...we hooked up and rolled out. There was some over 200 wagons, Captain Kennedy's train in front. Traveled up a canyon near a half mile and struck high rolling ground and the roads very dusty. Towards night, we camped on Raft River. Poor grass, having traveled 13 miles. Tonight at 12 o'clock E.J. Adams died from her wounds she received on Saturday last.

On August 12: "She was buried near Raft River by the side of G. W. Sanders from Keokuk, Iowa, who died here July 17, 1862, aged 33 years...At this place the road forked, the left hand leading to California. All the trains that left here today went that way except our own and a horse train of 25 wagons that stayed with us to Powder River..."

Counting the Dead

From the various authors of the events of August 1862 near American Falls, no certain account can be made of exactly how many were killed, how many wounded and who they were. No one account can be considered completely accurate. In 1927 the Sons of Idaho erected a monument in what is now Massacre Rocks State Park near the site of the massacres, reading as follows: "Massacre Rocks on Old Oregon Trail. In this defile on August 10, 1862, a band of Shoshone Indians ambushed an emigrant train bound for Oregon, killing nine white men and wounding six."

Even the marker legend was not totally accurate. The Indians actually attacked two trains about two miles apart, first the Smart train, then the Adams train and the date was August 9, not August 10, although some of the deaths occurred on August 10 in Kennedy's battle with the Indians. Moreover, Bert Webber in his book on the massacre counts the total number killed as ten.

Listed among those buried near the site of the massacre are: "A. J. Hunter and Masemo Lepi from the Smart train and George Adams, Charles Bullwinkel and George Shepard from the Adams train. Also, Elizabeth Adams, wounded in the first attack, died of wounds later and was buried near Raft River. Four were killed or missing in Kennedy's battle with the Indians, listed by McClung as George Leaper, George Adams (included above among the five buried at the scene of the attack), William Moats (spelling questionable), and Thomas Newman. Thus the total of nine seems to be the likely number killed. Henry Judson listed the names of ten wounded.

While the Shoshones were attacking wagon trains in Idaho on August 9, 1862, with no soldiers within hundreds of miles, the Union Army was in trouble in the East. General McClellan was in the process of evacuating his army from the Peninsula facing Richmond, after defeats against Lee's armies. Stonewall Jackson was shifting his Army of the Valley closer to Washington D.C. after defeating Union General Banks in the Shenandoah Valley. While the decision to strip most of the troops from the overland trails had been unavoidable, the War Department had provided a substitute of sorts.

Captain Medorem Crawford had been designated as Commanding Emigrant Escort. In the notice he posted to the emigrants, he advised them that he had been assigned to protect them. "The escort under my charge will consist of about fifty armed men. I shall leave Omaha about the 20th of May or as soon after as possible. My route will be up the Platte River, thence up the Sweetwater, over the Lander Road, leaving that road and crossing the Snake River a short distance this side of old Fort hall. There will doubtless be a ferry established for the convenience of the emigrants, in that vicinity...

"This escort is intended to protect emigrants as far as possible against Indian depredation, but unless emigrants will use the necessary precautions to insure their own safety, they are liable to suffer in spite of any assistance I shall be able to render them...."

In light of Captain Crawford's memo it seems fair to ask, where was Captain Crawford and his 50 armed men when the wagon trains were attacked on August 9? While we don't know exactly where he was, we do know that he was 22 trail days away from the site of the massacre. He arrived at the massacre site on August 31. After completion of his trip he wrote a report to the Secretary of War. One excerpt: "On the 31st of August, before reaching Raft River, we passed the graves of five men; from the inscription on the headboard of which we learned that they had been killed by Indians on the 9th, and immediately after crossing Raft River we found the grave of a Miss Adams, who was shot on the 9th and died on the 12th of August, doubtless belonging to the same party...."

After mentioning another later incident where an Indian had been killed and a white man wounded, he concluded: "These are all the evidences of Indian depredations that have come under my observation, and I am satisfied that many of the statements published on this subject are greatly exaggerated."

It seems that Crawford and his troops must have waited for all the emigrants to leave Omaha, then followed along well behind them. How that was of any benefit to the emigrants with the hostile Indian problem, is hard to see. While concluding that the published accounts of the attacks were "exaggerated", he does not himself attempt to report what happened or who did it, nor does he indicate any curiosity as to what did happened.

Moreover, he either did not see or ignored the evidence of other graves along the way of emigrants killed by Indians, as reported in some of the diaries. His self-serving report to the War Department seems designed to show that he had succeeded in his responsibility for the safety of the emigrants.

Perhaps the War Department didn't entirely dismiss the seriousness of the Indian attacks as Crawford's report would seem to do. They must have taken note of and given credit to some of the other reports. Six months later, Colonel Patrick Edward Connor's California volunteers responded in a punitive action that wiped out all the Indians in residence in a Shoshone winter camp. This included some Indians from Pocatello's group.

One other news account of the action should be mentioned. On October 4, 1862 the Washington

Statesman of Walla Walla, Washington Territory published what they labeled as part of the journal of one William Redhener. The lengthy narrative includes such sentences as "One of the party, named Bullwinkle, from New York City, was killed and robbed of between six and seven thousand dollars." The more I read the news story, the more familiar it seemed. I then realized that the excerpt attributed to Redhener was a word for word copy of entries from James McClung's diary.

The remarkable thing about the Redhener newspaper article was that McClung never went to Walla Walla. His destination was Western Oregon and the Redhener article, written by McClung was published while McClung was still traveling down the Columbia River towards his destination. We can assume that McClung must have made written copies of his account of the Indian battles and furnished one to Redhener. "Redhener" was probably the William Redheffler who was a member of the Kennedy train. It seems Redhener or Redheffler furnished McClung's account to the Washington Statesman and they attributed the account to him.

How great it would have been to interview Captain Medorum Crawford about the success of his Emigrant Escort service, safely getting the emigrants across the Overland Trail. Of course, we're too late and nobody ever interviewed him about his service, but this is what I imagine the course of such an interview would take.

Trailside interview with Captain
Medorum Crawford (as imagined):

Captain Crawford, how did your emigrant escort work out this year?

Crawford: Considering everything, our escort service worked out very well. We got several thousand people safely across the overland trail to Oregon and on the way we did a lot of trail repair, particularly on the Lander Cutoff, which had been badly damaged last winter.

When did you leave Omaha?

Crawford: I think it was the last few days of May. We had to wait till all the wagon trains had left.

I understand you mentioned the massacre at American Falls. How many emigrants were killed there?

Crawford: I think only five or six at most. There were some other reports, but they were greatly exaggerated.

Did you talk to any of the emigrants about that incident?

Crawford: No. We didn't get there until August 31. All the emigrants had gone on by then.

Did you talk to any Indians about the incident?

Crawford: Sir, when our troop arrived at the graves of the victims, the Indians were nowhere to be seen.

Captain, reports from the attacked wagon trains put the death toll at nine or ten and perhaps 10 wounded. Do you think they exaggerated?

Crawford: They like to make an interesting story out of any incident they encounter. Something to tell their grandchildren.

The journals of some of the emigrants note seeing a number of other graves of emigrants killed by Indians this year. Do you discount those reports?

Crawford: I'd like to see those reports. I saw no such graves on the trail.

Captain Crawford, if you left Omaha after all the wagon trains had gone ahead, and didn't catch up with any of them, how can you say you provided protection for the emigrants?

Crawford: Sir, I think our interview is over.

A Piece of His Scalp

After their battles with the Indians, burial of the dead and saying their goodbyes to the trains headed south to California, the Kennedy train leaving Raft River must have been a lonesome sight. They were still in hostile Indian country. The army was nowhere to be seen. None of the diarists gives us a count of the number of wagons in the train after Jane Gould counted 36 on July 28. If the count on August 12, as they left the California trains behind, was similar, that would be on the low side for safety in numbers.

One other small train continued west, camping near the Kennedy train. It was the Smart train, the horse train that had suffered the first Indian attack. Their numbers may have added a number of wagons to the size of the wagons traveling together, and added some safety.

John K. Kennedy, the intrepid leader of the train had proved himself in battle and was now a hero, even in the mind of James McClung, whose diary tends to side with the various groups of seceders, critical of Kennedy. Those seceders incidentally, had reached and passed unscathed through the massacre area prior to the attacks.

But Kennedy now lay severely wounded, by a poisoned arrow in one account. Two who wrote about his wound considered it mortal. While there were no body counts of the Indians killed in the battles, by all versions of events, many dead Indians were left on the ground. We can wonder whether Kennedy, whose son was killed by Indians, might have felt some satisfaction of payback.

McClung's mind, as the little group headed west, focused on the Indian danger, as usual. McClung was fascinated and repelled by Indians. He never missed telling of the graves of emigrants killed in Indian attacks and never failed to pass on evidence or rumors of Indian attacks, past, present, or future. Some of what McClung writes about seems to have been a little exaggerated, for example when he passes on estimates of numbers of Indians, height of natural curiosities and such. Moreover, the twenty-one year old farm boy may have been too credulous in passing on as fact, pretty much everything anyone tells him, particularly about Indians.

However, many of the incidents McClung recounts are things he saw himself, such as grave markers or evidence of posted notices along the trail or trashed and looted wagon trains. Even with discarding the rumors of Mormon complicity and the exaggeration of which he may have been guilty, the conclusion seems to be unmistakable that there were more Indian attacks and emigrant deaths from Indian attacks than have been verified historically, at least in the year 1862. 1862 was not a good year to cross the overland trails and McClung's journal verifies it. McClung didn't just make things up. There was certainly more evidence of deaths and incidents of Indian-emigrant violence in 1862 than Captain Medorem Crawford's report to the War Department admitted and there would be more to come.

On August 13 and August 15, McClung's diary gives us some evidence of two more incidents between the Indians and the emigrants. August 13: "Captain Kennedy not being able to travel, we were compelled to lay by. A company of the boys went out hunting. They found where they supposed a train had been massacred. They supposed they had gone off the road to get grass and water. The wagons were scattered in every direction and good trunks cut open and clothing was found in several places but no person was found..."

August 15: "Cloudy and rained in the forenoon which was thankfully received by us as the roads were four inches deep with dust. We soon crossed Goose Creek. Here we found a notice which stated that a train had been attacked here in the night by the Indians and had lost considerable stock and one man severely wounded and one Indian was found dead next morning."

The first of the two incidents, McClung passes on second-hand and could be exaggerated; also, there is no indication of how recently the incident occurred. However, about the second incident, McClung writes that 'we found a notice' telling of the second attack. Surely, here he is telling us of something that actually happened shortly before.

While the recent battles seem to have increased McClung's focus on Indian troubles, Hamilton Scott ignores the subject of Indian danger in his diary entries as the train moved west from Raft River on August 12, 1862. In fact, Scott makes no mention of Indians or Indian trouble for another eight days, when he will become personally involved in an Indian fight. Instead, he turns his attention back to the cattle on August 13. "Our cattle have become peaceful and healthy." It seems that the Kennedy train had finally learned how to keep their oxen from stampeding. How they had done it isn't completely clear, but apparently peaceful and healthy oxen do not stampede.

On Sunday August 17, Scott says "Had preaching by Father Paul." McClung added a little information as to the sermon. "...Mr. Paul delivered a sermon to us. His text was Romans 6th and 22nd. This is the second discourse we have had since we left the camp of rendezvous at Fremont..." Reverend Paul's text was: "But now that you have been set free from sin and have become slaves of God, the return you get is sanctification and its end, eternal life." The message that a better life awaited them after death must have been a great comfort to this little band of sorely tried and tired emigrants, who were still far from their destination.

James McClung's diary entry of August 16 writes of a fright, not mentioned by Scott. "Yesterday our horse train fell back and on Saturday morning a man from our train went back unknown to anyone to see what had become of the train. About noon, we missed him and a company started back in pursuit of him supposing the Indians had gotten him and, as I said before, we camped about 2 o'clock waiting from them to return. About dark, the men came in not having seen or heard of either Hatcher or the train."

The following day, good news: "Late this evening the company came up all safe and I can assure you there was great rejoicing on their arrival. We thought surely they were captured for during the day, Indians could be distinctly seen riding over hills about two miles from camp. However, at night pickets were placed out as usual. At about 11 o'clock, one of the pickets fired. This raised considerable of an excitement. In two minutes the whole company were ready for battle, but no enemy appeared. The picket stated something came slipping through the grass and raised up in ten feet of him and he supposed it was an Indian and he fired at it [and] it fell and he never seen or heard it anymore."

On August 20 men from the Kennedy train killed an Indian and Hamilton Scott was there and gives us a first hand, first person account of what happened. "The stock were herded on a branch of a creek in a deep canyon last night. There being a great many willows on the creek, one of the guards belonging to the horse train was shot in the arm by an Indian arrow. He was concealed in the willows. The men surrounded him and kept him until daylight, then they routed him. He made good use of his legs while the bullets whizzed after him. We ran him nearly two miles when he was shot down.

"I, being shorter of breath than some others, fell behind about a half mile. I did not go on to see him, but one of the boys gave me a piece of his scalp. The sun was now perhaps nearly one hour high and, as we were going on our way back to camp, we discovered what we took to be a heavy dust rising east of us which we concluded was a band of Indians who were coming to the rescue of their unfortunate comrade, which had fallen in our hands and whom was slain.

"You ought to have seen us go. I think we went back to camp in less time than we went out. However, as we neared the camp, we got brave and slowed down to a brisk walk. A little later, we discovered that it was only a fog or mist raising from the water, pouring over a falls on the Snake River."

Robert Scott later wrote an eye-witness account of the incident also: "...an Indian slipped up and shot one of the guards in the arm with an arrow. He gave the alarm to the other guards who sent word to our camp at once. The camp was wakened and the captain sent out 70 men to surround the canyon until sun rise, but they did not see the Indians. The Captain gave orders to go all through the rocks. We hunted about one and a half hours and were about to give up finding any Indians. Then one of the men found one Indian hiding under a rock in a hole near the top of the opposite side of the big hill where we camped.

"The Indian jumped up and ran. We followed shooting at him for about 2 miles before catching him. He had been shot about 16 times and was weakened from loss of blood and he fell. A young man named McQuire was nearest the Indian, shot all his ammunition into him and he still showed fight and McQuire struck him on the head with his six-shooter and killed him. We scalped him and left him laying there. I got some of the scalp. After we started back to camp and were one-half mile away, some other Indians came out and took him away, but we did not go after them, because we thought we got the one who shot our man and went on to camp..."

It's interesting to note that Robert Scott tells us they "thought" they got the right man. None of the accounts of the incident gives us the kind of details which would establish that the Indian the emigrants killed was the same one that shot an arrow into the guard.

McClung also gives us an account of the killing of the Indian on August 20, even though, again, he may not have been a participant. Some of his language here of the killing and the aftermath could be called colorful, even bloodthirsty. (McClung's diary shows the date as August 19, rather than August 20, and begins a period where either McClung's or the two Scotts' reckoning of dates is off by one day.) "Just as the morning star arose this morning, an Indian shot one of the guards. The arrow took affect in his right arm and came very near killing him. This caused another great excitement. Pickets were put out in every direction immediately for a half mile around camp.

"When daylight came, the guards closed in together and in some willows they found an Indian who had shot the guard. Here they killed him and scalped him and, I believe, he was the largest Indian I ever have seen. We then traveled on leaving him on the ground for his bones to bleach. I suppose we had not gone more than two miles when we saw several Indians hunting for him. We watched them until they found his body.

"Today, we traveled close to the river and could see Indians following us on the opposite side of the river and off in the mountains, we could see large smokes in every direction, which we supposed was a signal to call the tribe together to take their revenge for the life of the big Indian we killed. At noon we stopped on the bank to give our cattle water and take dinner. On the opposite side of the river we seen quite a number of warriors. They built a large fire out of some sage brush and then started on ahead of us, [on] horseback at full speed.

"We calculated it was their intention to cross the river ahead of us and attack us away from the river, as the road runs several miles from the river so we filled every bucket and canteen full of water and every man and every boy got their gun and fell into line and we moved on. We traveled some 12 miles and camped on Snake River, about dark without grass, where there was some Indians on the opposite side of the river fishing.

"Here a sprightly youth by the name of W. Joseph went to the river to get a bucket of water. About the time he got there and seen the Indians on the opposite bank, one of the boys in camp fired a gun, the echo sounding across the river. He thought the Indians were shooting at him. He dropped his bucket and ran into camp and said he saw 200 Indians across the river and they shot at him and struck the bank close by him. This caused considerable excitement among the women. Some went to praying and others to crying and others went to bed and did not get supper for their hands and when the guard was called on, the most of them were sick and others had to be appointed in their places."

While McClung took pains to squeeze every bit of drama possible from Indian fights and fears of future fights, Hamilton Scott told the story in a matter of fact fashion, not mentioning anything about the fear of Indian reprisal or the panic among the women. On several occasions McClung has noted the excitement and crying by the women in moments of fear. It is hard to believe these rugged pioneer women were quite as emotional as McClung leads us to believe.

To contrast Hamilton Scott's outlook, after participating in the killing of an Indian, and taking pride in receiving part of an Indian scalp, the very next day Scott tells us about trading with some friendly Indians. "Friendly Indians came to camp this morning with fish to trade; also, some came at noon. They tell us that we are out of the Snake tribe... We are near Salmon Falls."

On a diary entry McClung dates August 20, McClung says "...Captain Kennedy noticed his fine bull was missing and started two men back in search of him, while the train moved on and by the way, they had left a fine cow that he valued at $75, supposing when those two men came up, they would bring her in with them. We traveled five miles and camped on Snake River opposite Salmon Falls, having traveled 15 miles and no grass.

"Sometime after dark the two hands returned, not having seen or heard of the bull and, as they passed the place where the cow was left, they found him skinned alive, lying near the road. Here was hundreds of fresh Indian tracks, but no Indians to be seen. The boys said this made the blood stand cold in their veins, as they expected to be killed every minute."

Our Company Got Contrary

The following day, McClung records another lurid rumor of Indian treachery. "The Salmon Falls somewhat resembles the American Falls. Here were some Indians that seemed very friendly, but they had taken off a man that belonged to another train ahead of us. He was sitting on the bank of the river fishing after night. The company found his hat and boots the next morning but never seen him again. They heard he was burned to death."

It's hard to evaluate whether the event McClung described really happened. However, the fact that McClung was told such stories and recorded them in his diary, reflects the mind-set of the emigrants. Considering the actual Indian attacks they had experienced, it is not surprising that they were very ready to accept such reports as truthful.

After stopping for two days to rest their cattle, McClung records on August 24 starting out again, noting that "Our teams are very weak and the roads are four inches thick. We move tolerable slow. Traveled 7 miles and took dinner and grazed the stock on soft rushes and dry sage brush without water." Then he describes evidence of another Indian attack. "...we passed the place where there was a train captured 3 years since by the Indians. Here was the wagon irons and the wood work having all been burnt. The sheet iron stoves scattered about in every direction. We found several skull bones."

On August 25 McClung reports on a mutiny of sorts in the Kennedy train. "I will just say that our company got contrary and some refused to stand guard, so all the officers resigned their office. The company was called together by Buckskin Hall and organized over again, electing the same officers we had before and passed a law that the first man that refused to stand guard when called, unless sickness should prevent was to have his hands tied behind him and staked out 200 yards from camp overnight or be expelled from the train."

What the dispute was about or who the dissenters were, McClung doesn't tell us. Unfortunately, we have no cross-check with Hamilton Scott, nor does Robert Scott mention the affair in his later account. The incident provides another confirmation of Bernard DeVoto's assertion that 19th Century heads of families had an independent streak. "The captain's duties were large but his authority was theoretical; everyone had the inalienable privilege of dissent and especially of criticism."

Again, some members of the Kennedy train were disputing Kennedy's leadership. But the company was very aware of the fact that the train was still in hostile territory and the cavalry was nowhere to be seen. At least the majority of the company was willing to endure whatever faults they saw in Kennedy in return for his firm leadership. They were even willing to pass a "law", which would probably result in the death of any dissenter, to maintain Kennedy's control.

Finally, on August 27 James McClung makes a comment which could be interpreted as positive toward Indians. "In passing by along the bank of the river, I found an Indian canoe hid among the willow brush and [it] was one of the completest things I have ever seen."

Fort Walla Walla Saviors

It had now been more that four months since the Kennedy train left Fremont, Iowa and more than three months since they had left their last chance to stock up on provisions at the Missouri River crossing. Back at the Missouri River crossing, army Captain Medorem Crawford had advised the emigrants on the need to take all of the provisions they would need for the trip. "The time required from the Missouri River to the settlements will not vary much from one hundred days, with the teams...."

On August 28 it had been exactly 100 days since the Kennedy train had crossed the Missouri River and they were still far from settlements where provisions could be purchased. They were behind schedule and many were hungry. "Some of the company getting scarce of provisions and have been living on one biscuit a day while others are living on meat rinds that they saved for soap grease while we were traveling on the Platte River."

Margaret Stoot Thiel, Kennedy's step-daughter confirms that the company was running out of food before reaching their destination, even Kennedy's own family. "...our food supply began to get low, for we had been on the road nearly six months and we had expected to be on the road only four months. With nine in our party, including a bunch of hired men who were all jolly good fellows, our provisions got pretty short...Coffee, sugar, meat and tea all gave out and we paid $20 for a sack of flour."

There was one more hostile Indian incident as reported by McClung: "...we had not gone far when Orderly Standfield had an ox to get sick. Him and myself stayed back to doctor it. The train had got some 2 miles ahead of us when we seen an awful dust rising in the road, something like a half mile behind us.

"We knew it was not a train. The dust rising thicker and faster, we became rather uneasy. Presently we seen it was Indians on horseback and at full speed. Then they raised the yell and of all the yelling I ever heard, they done it then and we thought it best to be found taking care of our scalps. So we done some nice running and they after us, but they had nothing but bows and arrows and were afraid to come in reach of our guns, as we made signs to shoot. We soon caught up with our train, but did not tell how bad scared we were."

That same evening, August 28, 1862 reports: "We traveled 7 miles and came to Kyser Creek and here we met 300 soldiers from Fort Walla Walla. There was a good time of rejoicing when we met the soldiers. They were almost worshipped by our train. They furnished us with provisions of all kinds to see us through, while a great many would have perished if the government had not of given them assistance. Here we lay by from Friday noon till Wednesday the 3rd of September."

On to Oregon

While in camp under the protection of the cavalry soldiers from Fort Walla Walla, McClung reports catching salmon "from one to 3 feet long". Also, that "One half of the soldiers left Kyser Creek for Salmon Falls and the balance remained." Finally, he records a report of another very costly Indian attack.

"About 10 o'clock a train of 40 wagons came up and to our great joy and surprise, brought us 10 head of cattle that we lost in the stampede. On the night of the 26th of July, this train had a severe fight with the Indians beyond Fort Hall where 5 of their men were killed and several wounded. There were 10 packers (freight carriers) with them...

They were attacked near the same place. They fought half the day, 15 men against 200 Indians. Nearly all the pack animals were killed and several of the men wounded, but none killed. They finally made their escape. The wounded were taken to Salt Lake and the packers turned back when they met this train; and on their road back, they found 3 men near the road dead, supposed to be killed by the Indians."

This report by McClung is a bit confused, but it seems that he is reporting three separate attacks "beyond Fort Hall", in which a total of 8 men were killed and a number wounded. If these reports are true, Captain Crawford certainly missed some more important incidents of Indian-emigrant bloodshed in his summary to the War Department.

Perhaps on the strength of these new reports of Indian attacks, McClung notes that "Here our company tried to get an escort of Colonel Moor of 50 men, but he said he 'dare not divide my command as this is the most dangerous country, as they can raise 5000 warriors here in two hours notice at any time.'"

Both the Scott and McClung diaries note that the Kennedy train again started west again on September 3rd and on the following day we note that McClung is still carefully recording every instance of Indian difficulties. "...for 6 miles we traveled near the river (The train had been traveling not far from the south bank of the Snake River for nearly a month.), where the youngsters devoted their time in fishing . I noticed some young ladies setting on the bank of the river enjoying themselves finely as they were pulling out the fish. When two Indians came riding along they threw their fishing poles and left their fish and took to their heels and the Indians laughing at them." Perhaps McClung is conceding here that the girls had over-reacted in their fear of the two Indians.

On September 9, the two diaries both report arrival at the Owyee River which is just inside Oregon. They are no longer in Idaho. But they are still far from the first settlement. By September 12 at a high altitude they both note the cold weather. Scott says "our overcoats did not come amiss." McClung says: "Cold, windy and spitting snow. Very disagreeable."

On September 10 and 11, Robert Scott's journal reported a serious problem with the stock, not noted in other accounts. On the 10th, he noted that they had found no grass or water all day and the stock are "very weak and hungry. We think it best to drive some tonight and avoid the heat. We hitched up at 5 p.m. and drove 12 miles, then made a dry camp, that is, without grass or water, stock suffering and almost given out. We had to stop, they could not go on."

Then on the 12th: "We started this a.m. at daylight. The cattle are bellowing and horses nickering for water and feed. We were becoming afraid of them. [It] had been a day and night without feed or water. This was a terrible predicament to be in. We managed to get on about 10 miles and come to a small stream. When near the river, the stock smelled the water and we could hardly handle them. When close enough, we quickly unhitched them and they ran for water. We could not control them any longer. We were afraid they would kill themselves by drinking so much. Then they went for grass. We stayed here until morning and got filled up, stock rested awhile, then drink and eat again, by morning they were satisfied."

On September 13, now getting closer to settlements, probably not now worried about Indian attacks, they report the last "falling out" with Kennedy. Hamilton Scott: "Captain Kennedy resigned this morning and the company is well pleased because he did." Hamilton Scott's brother Robert, in writing about the trip later added a little more about Kennedy's resignation: "Our people had become dissatisfied with him and asked him to resign, because of his overbearing attitude. All seemed to be glad of his resignation." Hamilton Scott added that, "He and his men that he furnished with teams camped by themselves this evening. We understand that we have been in Oregon for forty-five miles but we are sixty-five miles from settlement yet. The first settlement is on Powder River. They are gold miners."

Hamilton Scott's mention of 'men that he furnished with teams' can perhaps be explained by the newspaper interview with his step-daughter many years later. In a 1926 newspaper article, Margaret Stoot Thiel was quoted to say: "My stepfather, John Kennedy sold our place in Mahaska County, Iowa and turned all of our property into money. Nine other families near us wanted to come west, so they promised that if my stepfather would buy wagons and oxen for them and outfit them to cross the plains, they would return the money he spent with good interest, when they got to Oregon. He outfitted these nine families. When they got out there, they promised him that if they ever got any money ahead that they could spare, they would pay him what they owed, but he never got a cent from them."

James McClung's diary of September 14 tells us of John Kennedy's resignation the previous day. "I forgot to say that yesterday Captain John K. Kennedy, the honorable Devil fell out with the company and we drove off leaving him behind and last night he camped with the horse train within 300 yards of our camp so this morning he, with a few others drove on leaving the horse train and ours behind, so about 9 o'clock we rolled on. We had gone but a short distance when we saw they had corralled. Supposing we were going to remain in camp, thought it best to not venture too far. When they seen we were coming they rolled on."

While some of the above language isn't too clear, it does clearly indicate that the break between Kennedy and the majority of the train was not a friendly one. It seems they were uncomfortable even camping near each other. Also the use of the term "honorable devil" is interesting. In the Nineteenth Century the word 'devil' was very profane and to call someone a devil was probably considered more powerful language than it would be today.

The Oregon State Historical Society Archives hold two versions of McClung's diary. Both are hand-written originals, perhaps both copied shortly after the trip from a record McClung made while on the trail. The two documents were written in different hands, but are almost identical, word for word, except for variable spelling. However, in one of the two manuscripts, the writer seems to have deliberately balked at writing that profane word 'devil', but simply writes: "John K. Kennedy the honorable _____", much as editors now substitute 'bleep' for what they consider an unprintable word.

It's difficult to comprehend what James McClung really thought of Kennedy. His attitude seems to vary. Early in the trip there is some indication that he is interested in one of Kennedy's daughters. Later, while cautiously reporting defections from the company, he is critical of Kennedy, saying he is "never satisfied" and it seems like he would have preferred to leave the Kennedy train and go with them. Later, he seems to be sympathetic to Kennedy's part in the 'dog law' flap.

After the Indian attack he praises Kennedy's role without limit: "...acted the part of a man and proved himself worthy..." However, when Kennedy finally resigns, he is ready to call him 'devil', at the time, probably a fighting word. To find out what McClung 'really thinks of Kennedy', perhaps we should wait to hear the invective he aims at Kennedy in his letter home after he is safe and sound in the Willamette Valley. It's just speculation, but McClung may have been sharing his diary with others on the trip, inducing a toning down of what he writes about Kennedy. We know he shared his diary with Redheffler (or Redhener), who was credited with McClung's account of the Indian attack in the Walla Walla Statesman on October 4, 1862. Perhaps he shared his diary widely among the company.

Hamilton Scott gives us a little more information about the split on September 15. "Drove twelve miles. Camped still on the same stream. There were high mountains on both sides of us. We have now twenty-one in our company. We have elected Mr. Hall as our Captain."

This is the first fix on the number of wagons in the train for some time. Starting from Fremont, Iowa there were about a dozen wagons, to be joined by a few more after they reached the Missouri. When the company was organized, just after the crossing they had 52. After Independence Rock the count was 80. After two major defections and some stampedes, Jane Gould counted 36, with the loss of only one wagon noted after that. After Kennedy resigned as Captain, he was left with the parties he had financed, nine, if his step-daughter's account is correct, and the remaining company of 21 wagons was now captained by Buckskin Hall.

It's hard to escape the conclusion that the majority of the Kennedy train company were more than willing to stick with Kennedy and whatever his faults were as long as there was a fear of Indian attacks. They seemed to have great confidence in Kennedy's ability to secure the safety of the train, but now that the danger was seen to have passed, they were very glad to get out from under his authority. Still, McClung again brings our attention to the fear of Indian attacks on September 14.

"...we came in a canyon with a dense thicket on each side with barely room for a wagon to pass through. Here the Independent Braves took their position on each side, passing through the middle as we were expecting an attack..."

On September 16, McClung notes coming into an area where people are mining gold and meets an old friend. "...we passed places where miners were prospecting for gold. We crossed one creek where the water was very swift and was very muddy. This we thought very strange from the fact mountain streams are always clear and beautiful. However, we afterwards learned there was miners at work a few miles above and making big wages...we camped on Burnt River, where our old friend Mr. Ed Culberson (McClung's spelling) and some of his company that left us at Green River met us tonight as they were going back a prospecting. There was quite a time of rejoicing. They stated they had been through a month and had very good luck."

It seems doubtful that the Culberson train could have arrived at this point in the trail a month ahead of the Kennedy train. If they did, they had very good luck indeed. This seems like an exaggeration.

The Roads Part

Hamilton Scott's last diary entry was dated September 18. It records his departure from the wagon train. "Five miles brought us to where the roads part, one leading to Fort Walla Walla and the other to Powder River gold mines ten miles from Auburn."

A note by Alvin Zaring, a member of Scott's party whose descendants owned the copy of Scott's diary published in 1949, finishes the trip to Walla Walla. "After the last date mentioned, September 18, there was no diary kept while on the road to Walla Walla. We had nice weather, good grass and water. We passed through La Grande, Oregon which had only a few houses. I paid 10 cents a pound for potatoes here. We had no accidents or trouble from Powder River to Walla Walla which took us nine days to travel. On the 27th of September, we struck our last camp six miles southeast of Walla Walla on Cottonwood Creek."

McClung also records the parting of the roads on September 18. "A pleasant morning. We started by sunrise and traveled 3 miles and came to the road which leads to Auburn City, near the gold mines on Powder River. Here [we stayed] at the forks of the road for several hours. Some were going to stop at Auburn City, which was 15 miles distant from here and here the company divided, some going that road and some the other. As we left here, our train was quite small.

"Captain Bristoe's horse train stopped here. I must confess, we felt lonesome and bad as we bid adieu to friends that had crossed the extended plains with us; that had stood by us in the hour of danger and had traveled together for 5 months. They seem dear to us indeed and many a tear was shed at our separation. From here the road was level and nice for 14 miles to where we struck Powder River. It is a small creek 2 rods wide. Here we camped and turned the stock out till morning without guards." Finally, McClung recognizes that the danger of Indian attack has passed, but still tells us that "we rose early and found the stock all right."

On September 20 McClung reaches the Grande Ronde Valley. "We rolled on for 5 miles raising the tip of a high mountain which overlooked Grande Ronde Valley. Here our eyes beheld one of the most beautiful valleys in the known world. It is surrounded by mountains and is 15 miles in width and 35 miles in length. We descended gradually from the mountain tip to this beautiful valley...We camped near here about 2 hours by sun having traveled 15 miles today."

Having arrived at something like civilization, on the 21st, McClung tells us that "...we lay by today, some of the company wishing to look around and see the valley. Here we bought some beef and mutton. We paid 15 cents per pound, the first we have had and I believe it was the best meat that I ever ate. There is one company of soldiers stationed here and there are a good number of emigrants stopping here and taking claims."

Monday, September 22, 1862 "...we came to La Grande City, five houses, one store and a blacksmith shop. Flour is selling at $20 per hundred and everything in proportion. Some of the people were living in their tents and wagon beds until they could build houses....we struck the foot of the Blue Mountains, which are covered with high lofty timber, pine and fir...we camped on Grande Ronde River, which is 2 rods wide and one foot deep."

On the 23rd and the 24th the little group of wagons were ascending the Blue Mountains and reached Lee's Encampment, now Meacham, Oregon. "Here was plenty of water but there were several pack trains who had possession of the grazing ground, so we rolled on four miles farther and camped near a small spring."

On September 25 the train reached the summit of the Blue Mountains and had done so before the high winter snowfalls, which would make the trail impassable. They had passed the last hurdle. McClung records the sight. "We came to the top of the last Blue Mountain. Here we could see as far as our eyes could reach over a level plain without timber...from here we descended to the foot of the mountain, which was three miles..."

From many locations on top of the Blue Mountains, a person can see as 'far as our eyes could reach'. On some very clear days, you can see all of the snow capped volcanic peaks of the Cascade Mountains: Mt. Hood, Mt. St. Helens, Mt. Adams, Mt. Rainer and even Mt. Baker, three hundred miles away, near the Canadian border.

On the same day, September 25, the little group split again, near what is now Pendleton, Oregon, the majority going on to Walla Walla. "Here we bid adieu to some more of our friends as they were intending to go to Walla Walla Valley, which was only 40 miles distant and we, with several families rolled on for the Willamette Valley."

Two days later, Saturday, September 27, 1862, the remainder of the little group, now led by Buckskin Hall, arrived in Walla Walla. Kennedy himself didn't continue on to Walla Walla. According to his step-daughter, "Father took up a claim on 160 acres near La Grande..." It is supposed that the little group that had stayed with Kennedy also went on to Walla Walla, also arriving about September 27. Robert Cummins, who had left the Kennedy train on July 30 to join the Culberson train, wrote later of arriving in Walla Walla on September 28, 1862.

Heading down the Columbia three days after saying goodbye to the Walla Walla bound emigrants, McClung ended his diary on September 30. He started his last diary entry in his characteristically flamboyant language. "Raining like gee whilaker and cold as gee whiz." He ends the final diary day with, "...we took what meat rinds we had saved for soap grease and used them for fuel, which made the old stove move things right through. To be continued." Then: "Written by James S. McClung and sent to his mother Mrs. Mary E. McClung of Dahlonega., Wapello County and State of Iowa."

His comment that the diary was "to be continued" seems to refer to the letter he wrote to his mother after arrival at his destination in the Willamette Valley. In that letter, he continues to record the day to day events of the remainder of the trip as well as adding some private comments about Kennedy and the Kennedy train he failed to record in his diary.

It seems almost unfair that most of what we now know about the Kennedy train traces back to the journals of two young men, James McClung and Hamilton Scott, and the aging memories of a few others. Apparently nothing of what Kennedy himself thought about the trip and his associates has survived.

Certainly it would be fair to at least speculate on what Kennedy would say, if given the chance. Perhaps if interviewed, he may have said something like the following:

Mr. Kennedy, what made you decide to settle in the Grande Ronde Valley?

Kennedy: It's a great area and I've located some property that I think will be a very good situation for me. Also, I must say, I was ready for the trip to end and my wound told me to travel no farther.

Do you have any regrets that you took the leadership of the train? Some of the people seem to have given you a very bad time.

Kennedy: I think it would have been all right if we'd kept the train down to just my outfit and a few close neighbors and relatives. But we couldn't do that. We had to have a much bigger train for safety. Remember, it was just those two small trains that the Indians attacked at American Falls. But those strangers we took on, and some of my neighbors too, just didn't want to follow orders. I had no idea some of those farmers were so contrary.

I understand some of the people that split off from your train were very critical of the way you talked to some of the emigrants. Were they right?

Kennedy: They were way too sensitive. Some of them talked to me the same way or worse, always criticizing and finding fault with every decision I made. They even arranged it so I had to kill my own dog. They came close to mutiny, time and again. Then, when there was danger they said, "Where is Kennedy? Find Kennedy!" I am sick of them and for most of them, if I never see them again that will be just fine.

175

I understand young James McClung was pretty upset with you. What happened?

Kennedy: I don't want to talk about that worthless young man. Whenever there was work to be done, what was he doing? Writing in his diary! His boss should have got rid of him. He got it into his head that one of my daughters was his girlfriend. I changed his mind about that. I don't wonder he writes bad things about me in his journal.

How do you think those farmers that went on to the Walla Walla area will fare?

Kennedy: They'll do fine. They are good farmers and they will find miles and miles of unbroken top-soil six feet deep. It's good country. They can't miss. By the way, thank you for stopping by and giving me a chance to give my side of the story. I wasn't sure anybody was interested.

While the above may or may not have been Kennedy's view of the trip, it doesn't seem fair that Kennedy has had no opportunity to rebut the criticism of those who kept journals.

James McClung's Letter Home

Safely arrived in Lane County Oregon, McClung wrote a letter to his father and mother in Iowa, dated October 24, 1862. Some excerpts follow. "... started over the Cascade Mountains down the Columbia River with the cattle. The distance was near 200 miles through the worst mountains I ever saw and inhabited by nothng but bears and wild savages..."

After arriving in Portland, McClung gives some observations about the city. "Portland City is about 6 times as big as Ottumwa (a small city near Dahlonega) and on the Willamette River, about 12 miles from where it empties into the Columbia [140?] miles from the coast, but ships run up as far as Portland. There was one come while we was there. About Portland, the country is very rough and mountainous...

"We remained here several days, then bought one yoke of cattle and started up the Willamette Valley, which is called the garden spot of Oregon. It is flat lowland and was all overflowed with high water last winter. Some houses was entirely washed off. Lots of families drowned. Coming along it was hard work to buy oats or hay at any price to feed 5 head of stock. The fences was all washed off and not repaired. The farmers all left their farms and went to the mines and came home strapped. So this makes hard times here.

Oregon is a good country for fruit. Apples is plenty and some peaches. The fine timber cannot be beat nowhere. But the oak is low and scrubby as the Iowa timber. This is called the best portion of Oregon and I like some of the valley very well and I think if we had some of the Iowa farmers here instead of these old Oregonians, it would be much better."

McClung continues, discussing his contacts with mutual friends and relatives from Iowa, then lets his hair down and records some of the things he now wants to tell his family and the folks at home, but did not want to put in his diary. Some of his comments go well beyond exaggeration.

"Now, how we crossed the plains. As you are aware, we started in company with the honorable Captain J. K. Kennedy, who proved to be one of the meanest men unhung. This is so. He was drunk the whole time; could out-swear any man I ever saw and told more lies than any liar ever did. He turned [out?] several families on the plains without any cause and with nothing. Our train was two months longer a crossing than others. It is true our cattle was stampeded several times, which caused a great deal of trouble, but that was nothing.

"By being on the road so long he run out of flour for one week. They lived on a biscuit a meal and lots [of] others. Some that saved their meat rinds for soap grease on Platte River before they got through ate them and was glad to get them. For ourselves, we faired well and divided with those that had none...."

James McClung's letter to his parents seems to have been written hurriedly, seeming to leave words out at times and some of his handwriting is not as careful as his diary entries. It's doubtful McClung anticipated this particular letter would be handed down to generations and centuries to come. Still, the very closing passage of his letter, a kind of PS, probably expresses his true views better than anything he wrote in his diary.

"I have not got into business yet and do not know what I shall do this winter. Write soon. Direct your letters to Lane County, Pleasant Hill, Oregon. If I have any friends in Iowa, if they know how to appreciate a good living, stay there until the Indians is all killed and the war-paths ground up and their wigwams scattered like a sheep's wool on a brush fence...J. S. McClung."

McClung's statement that the Kennedy train took two months longer than other trains, simply is not true. Captain Medorem Crawford indicated it should take about 100 days from the Missouri to the first settlements. The Kennedy train reached La Grande in about 115 days. Moreover, much of the additional time can be attributed to the Indian attacks in Idaho, including delays due to Kennedy's serious wounds.

As to the other serious charges McClung levied on Kennedy, of drunkenness, lies, and the abandonment of people, perhaps to die on the plains, none of the other accounts, either at the time nor from survivors later, ever noted any of those deficiencies. Even though many in Kennedy's train took issue with him, or disputed his orders at times and many seceded from his company, when danger was apparent, they all instinctively looked to Kennedy for leadership and he provided it. Even members of nearby trains looked to Kennedy for action and leadership when something had to be done about a murderer and when Indians attacked.

Something must have happened between young James McClung and John Kennedy to account for the invective McClung directed at Kennedy in his letter to his mother. Early in the trip, McClung reports visiting an Indian village "in company of some young ladies...the old chief came out and seeing a beautiful intelligent girl by the name of Miss Kennedy, he was determined to have her. But she claimed she was mine and could not stay..." It's not too great a leap of conjecture to believe McClung had a romantic interest in the "beautiful Intelligent girl by the name of Miss Kennedy."

In the very same diary entry, McClung wrote favorably about a couple from another train who were married by Reverend Paul. He concluded his entry with the comment: "So you see, people can marry on the plains as well as at home..." McClung never mentioned Kennedy's daughter again. Something must have happened, a rebuff from the daughter or from Kennedy himself to prompt the fury of McClung's comment to his mother.

Disregarding McClung's intemperate remarks about Kennedy and, in the absence of facts as to why Kennedy lost the confidence of the majority of his company, we're left simply with the presumption his demanding discipline and rigidity turned off the members of his company. Yet they selected him for those very qualities and stood by him and sought the protection of his discipline throughout the dangerous part of the trip. When the danger was seen to subside, they no longer needed his firm leadership and turned to a gentler leader.

One Kennedy train researcher also wondered why Kennedy was ousted. Pat Packard told me she concluded it was because of "camp fever", that is, several hundred people, too close together for four months of hardship, simply were ready and overdue for a change.

Kennedy's ouster was perhaps analogous to Winston Churchill's election defeat at the end of World War II. When danger passed, England and the Kennedy Company were ready for a change.

In their reconstruction of the Kennedy roster, researchers Pat Packard and Marjorie Ellis Miles noted something rare about the Kennedy Company. "In later years, most former emigrants recorded themselves simply as having crossed the plains. Veterans of the Kennedy Company added, 'with the John K. Kennedy Company'..." They also noted that the Kennedy train came to the rescue of trains in trouble, "something not all wagon trains would have done. The Kennedy Company understood that civilization doesn't come cheap."

After the trip, Kennedy resumed his life much as he had lived it In Iowa, first farming in the Grande Ronde valley in Oregon. By 1864 or 1865 he and his wife Sarah were living in Walla Walla County, Washington Territory. He moved to a farm near Dayton, Washington in Columbia County in 1872. There he was again affiliated with the local Masonic Lodge. Kennedy died June 25, 1889 and was buried in Waitsburg, Walla Walla County, Washington. His wife Sarah died the following year.

James S. McClung found employment during his first year in Oregon as a school teacher. According to descendants of his relatives, James McClung never married and died in a mining accident in Butte, Montana in 1889.

Little is known about Hamilton Scott, who left the Kennedy train at the Powder River gold mines. The International Genealogical Index of the LDS Church shows Scott's death as 1865, but does not indicate where he died or the source of the information.

Bringing their Iowa farming skills with them, the nucleus of the Iowa farm families – the Kennedys, Cummins', Ellis', Zarings, Pauls, McGuires, Taylors, Files and others – settled on land in and around Walla Walla and Southeastern Washington, raising grain and cattle. Their plows turned over the deep, rich, previously undisturbed topsoil Kennedy had told them about, helping the area become one of the principal wheat growing areas in the United States.

Robert Cummins About 1876

John Knox Kennedy And His Wife Sarah

Appendix 1

"Reconstruction of Roster of 1862 Kennedy Company, John K. Kennedy, Captain" by Pat Packard and Marjorie Ellis Miles; Idaho Genealogical Quarterly, April 1993. The following is a partial list of emigrants who are believed to be members of the 1862 Kennedy Company.

I have omitted the names of family members from the roster and only listed names of emigrants who may have been heads of families or independent travelers. While this roster is far from complete, many first names not available and the spellings uncertain, this list of emigrants, compiled by Pat Packard and Marjorie Ellis Miles, may be as complete a list as has been compiled for any Oregon-bound wagon train.

Marjorie Ellis Miles has the distinction of being descended from three Kennedy train emigrants. Ellis Ebenezer Ellis and Eliza Jane Zaring Ellis were her great-grandparents and their son Charles, born along the Sweetwater River during the trip was her grandfather. Also, Mary Elizabeth Paul Maxson was her great-grandmother; and the Reverend Joseph Paul and Mary Cummins Paul were her great-great grandparents.

Algoods
Arthing
Bailey, G. W.
Bovee, George
Bowell
Bowman
Clark, Fred
Collins, Dr. D. Y.
Coons, W. H.
Creamer, J. W.
Culberson, Ed
Cummins, Robert
Cunningham
Deitrich
DeLong
Dole
Ellis, Ellis E.
Espsy
Files, Robert
Forebush
Gholson
Goyer
Hale
Hall, Buckskin
Hathaway

Hill, Stephen
Hoover
Hunter, A.
James, Joseph W.
Kennedy, John K.
Little
Macky/MacKay, Thomas
Mard
Mateker
McClung, James
McCormick
McGuire, John Garrett
Miller, Abram/Augustus
Neely
Newman, Tom
Ocherman
Orndorf
Paul, Rev. Joseph
Paul, Rev. Thomas
Piper
Raley, Johnathan
Rayburn
Redheffler/Redhener, William
Rounceville, Nathan
Russell

Scott, Hamilton
Scott, Robert
Scott, Wison
Slater
Smales
Standfield, James
Taylor, Ephraim
Towndsend
Scott Vennerns
Zaring, Alvin

Appendix 2

Martha McGuire Fitzsimmons Narrative: "Pioneer Daughters Thrilled by Talks", East Washingtonian, Pomeroy, Washington, November 12, 1942

Mrs. Martha Fitzsimmons was a distinguished guest at the meeting of the Daughters of the Pioneers at the home of Mrs. Bill Kuykendall Monday evening as was also Mrs. Nettie Long. Both Mrs. Fitzsimmons and Mrs. Long told of pioneer experiences and held the rapt attention of the younger people present during their storytelling, in the flickering light of the fireplace in the Kuykendall cabin.

"I was born on November 14, 1852 in Ottumwa, Wapello County, Iowa, and came west with my parents, Mr. and Mrs. John Garrett McGuire, when I was 10 years of age. My father had long planned going to the west and organized a pioneer emigrant train of covered wagons, 60 of them, and his wife and family of eight children started out. The train was captained by my uncle John Kennedy.

"It took six months to reach Walla Walla, and on the trip there were plenty of hardships. Day after day, week after week, month after month there was nothing but sagebrush, greasewood and prairie sand. We would sleep, ride and walk again and again, for miles and miles.

"The cattle often got frightened at night and stampeded. One ox team ran away and killed the occupant of the wagon, an expectant mother. She was buried on the prairie. Her little boy, now orphaned was taken along, and had to be cared for.

"In our party was a Dr. Collins. He was called on frequently for various ailments and to care for the arrival of new babies, but Captain Kennedy's wife was the midwife, and attended to her duties when occasion demanded, while the wagons went rumbling along.

"Often the plains were marked with an occasional solitary mound with a slab of wood or stone. One day some of the men in the party caught sight of a dead man half buried in the ground, feet sticking out. Murder was immediately suspicioned, and a man known to be a hard character in the wagon train ahead was suspected. A group went ahead and arrested the fellow and he was brought back, tried and convicted. They led him off to shoot him out of sight of the women and children. I recall seeing the poor fellow taken away.

"We hungered for fresh fruit and vegetables, and used to eat the buds or seed pods of wild roses. Sometimes the cattle got sore feet and the train would have to halt and remain for awhile until the cattle were able to go on. These delays were vexing to all, who wished to go on. Sometimes camp was made at night, with no water near for human or stock use. These were called dry camps. Water that was carried in cans for such emergencies was always warm and insipid.

"In camping, the wagons were placed in a circle and the emigrants and cattle were placed inside, with men on guard at night. Sometimes the cattle stampeded, in spite of all precautions and got away, making it necessary for the men to chase them and bring them back. Once in awhile one of the cattle died along the way, making it necessary to leave buggies, hacks, saddles or furniture, when draft power of the remaining animals became so depleted that these could not be taken.

"I was riding along one day with my cousin, Jane Neely," continued Mrs. Fitzsimmons, "when word came back that a small train with but a few wagons and drawn by horses had been attacked by the Indians, and that the emigrants were killed.

"Scouts were sent out, and came upon the massacred party at noon time. Wagon sheets had been ripped off the covered wagons, trunks broken open, and feathers from the feather beds scattered for miles over the prairie. Everything of value had been taken by the Indians. Our train camped there while some of the men went to try to find and punish the Indians. Some of the men never returned. Captain John Kennedy was wounded by a poisoned arrow. The place where that killing occurred is now known as Massacre Rock, and is near American Falls, Idaho.

"At La Grande, Oregon we came to the first house we had seen for months and with women in it. Most of us had forgotten how it seemed to live in a house."

The McGuires reached Walla Walla valley in the fall of 1862. The most impressive thing Mrs. Fitzsimmons remembers was the cabbage bought for the family by her father, upon arriving there.

The McGuires located on Russell Creek, southeast of Walla Walla and the old house which they built is still standing.

Martha Jane McGuire married Charles Wesley Fitzsimmons, in the old McGuire homestead, November 7, 1875. He was born in Kirkville, Iowa, February 15, 1850. He came west in 1873. The Fitzsimmons moved to what is Garfield County in May 1879 and located on Alpowa ridge, taking up land which is now farmed by their son, Stanley Fitzsimmons. Mr. Fitzsimmons passed away November 1, 1938.

Appendix 3

Mary Elizabeth Paul Maxson Article: "Wagon Train Emigrant Here Since 1862 Has Anniversary", October 1942 Walla Walla Union-Bulletin Article

The history of a long and eventful life was recounted Saturday on the occasion of the ninety second birthday anniversary of Mrs. Mary Elizabeth Maxson, who crossed the plains in 1862.

Mrs. Maxson was born in Mahaska County, Iowa, October 4, 1850. When she was five years old a cholera epidemic swept the country taking her father and maternal grandmother within a week of each other.

Four years later, her mother married again and the family moved to Wapello County.

It was about this time that the western trek was in full swing and in April 1862 the McGuire family joined a train of a dozen wagons to cross the plains.

This group journeyed as far as Omaha where they spent four weeks waiting for enough more to make a safe crossing in the face of Indian trouble and other perils.

Finally, 200 wagons had collected and what is known as the Kennedy train, the largest ever to come West, set forth on the long pilgrimage.

The trip consumed six months, the party arriving here in late September.

Births, marriages and deaths featured the trek. Mrs. Maxson remembers the heartbreaking farewells of a pair of sweethearts. Refusing to be left behind, the girl overtook the party after following for many miles on foot and the wedding resulted.

The outdoor life agreed with children who had been frail and others, both old and young sickened and died as a result of the hardships.

The road was a single track cut deep by the hundreds of wagon wheels and the line of march was arranged with the slower ox teams leading and the mule and horse drawn wagons following, Mrs. Maxson explains.

Each covered wagon was equipped with a loaded gun and ammunition but the party was fortunate in evading Indians. Only one who lurked about the train for several days, was shot.

Wagons abandoned along the way by less fortunate travelers, were substituted by those following if they were in better repair than their own.

Justice was meted out to those causing trouble in the party. Mrs. Maxson recollects the train coming upon a man's body half buried in a rocky grave and the pursuit of the murderer and his trial by jury.

He was convicted and given his choice of death by hanging, drowning or a firing squad with the guilty one choosing the latter.

Two things Mrs. Maxson says she never will forget, the prisoner's cries all through the night and the sight of him sitting on his coffin facing the firing squad and his subsequent fall as the fatal shot was fired.

Green River in Wyoming was at flood stage and the party was forced to camp there for some time until the oxen could be taken across.

The wagon beds were calked and fastened high on the standards and with the oxen pulling a series of chains attached to them, the women and children were ferried across the river.

The train stopped every Saturday noon but three when water was not available. Repairs were made, washing and baking were done in preparation for the next week's journey.

Mrs. Maxson's mother brought two milk cows which, incidentally, worked with the oxen the while furnishing plenty of milk and butter, the churning done en route by the motion of the rough riding wagons.

The oxen, though slower, stood the trip much better than the horses and mules, she states.

At Boise the party separated, many choosing to go south to California.

The McGuire family settled on Russell Creek buying land at $1.25 an acre. Others homesteaded and some took timber culture claims.

There were no roads and the family drove over open country to church in Walla Walla, a town of about 200 inhabitants, relates Mrs. Maxson.

When she was 15 years old, she married Sam R. Maxson, 19, who had come west in 1859. They moved into a log cabin which is still standing and which provided the nucleus for the present modern home of the late John W. McGuire, Mrs. Maxson's brother.

Mrs. Maxson remembers bursting into tears when a series of snaps from newspapers which they had painstakingly pasted over the interior of the log house, cracked into shreds. Mrs. Maxson lived in this log house for 40 years.

The Maxson schoolhouse was the first school in that part of the valley. The land was donated by her father-in-law. The first building was of logs, the second of frame construction and the present building is concrete.

Through all these years, it has been a veritable community center. Revival meetings and church services, singing school and spelling bees have been held there.

Mrs. Maxson, who still reads headlines without benefit of glasses, has never missed an issue of the local newspaper since she has been here.

First it was the Walla Walla Weekly Statesman, then the Walla Walla Union and now the Union-Bulletin.

She has been a member of the Methodist church for 77 years.

Mrs. Maxson is in perfect health and until the last year has attended church regularly. She writes six or seven letters a week and always a good speller, acts as the family dictionary to this day.

Her husband died 33 years ago. The Maxsons had 12 children, six of whom are living.

They are Charles Maxson, Russell Creek; Mrs. May Harris, Trenton, Mo; Stephen Maxson, Fern and Pleasant Streets, with whom she makes her home; Mrs. Myrtle Swezea, Seattle; Walter Maxson, Walla Walla; and Ralph Maxson, Stauffer, Alberta.

There are 20 grandchildren, 18 great-grandchildren and two great-great grandchildren.

Appendix 4

Christena Taylor Chambers: "Covered Wagons Real to Her", Portland Oregonian Sunday Magazine, February, 1950, Story by free-lance writer, Philip O. Olsen

Mrs. Chistena Chambers of Lewiston, Idaho, usually called Aunt Teen, is 92 years old. She doesn't have to read books and try to imagine what pioneer life was like. She knows.

When "Teen" was 5, her parents, Ephraim and Nancy Taylor, started from Iowa in May 1862. They had oxen and two covered wagons. There were eight children, and two men traveled with them. A neighbor, John K. Kennedy, led a train of 62 wagons.

Likely they followed the Mormon Trail north of the Platte River and joined the Oregon Trail near Fort Kearney in south central Nebraska.

Cows were brought along. Cream in a crock in the wagon made butter during a day's jolting. Hot biscuits were baked almost every morning in a reflector oven. Raised bread was baked when a stop was made for clothes washing. There always was food for all, though some of the bacon was crammed down the throats of oxen poisoned by alkali.

Boys old enough to stand guard with the men were very proud. One of the men scoffed at the boys. When it was his turn to watch he went to sleep. The boys dragged him down into a creek and laughed all the way to Oregon.

Teen's mother went to the first trading post, but there were no fresh vegetables except one 4 pound onion. The trader made her a present of it.

Aunt Teen remembers only two trading posts. The other may have been at Fort Laramie, in Wyoming, or Fort Hall, Idaho. She says they did not see any buffalo.

On July 6 there was a murder. Two men with a mule team had joined the train. The younger man shot the little old man who owned the outfit, but did not get him buried before the train came up.

A jury of 12 men assembled in a rough enclosure of logs. A fire was kept going, and the accused man was there under guard. Children clambered on logs and others drew near and listened. The sentence was death by shooting. The man had little to say for himself except that he didn't know there was any harm in killing a man on the plains. He had a family back east and spent most of the night writing letters.

In the morning the oxen were yoked and the train prepared to move. A firing squad of 12 men was ready, some of the rifles carrying blank loads. A grave had been dug and a coffin made of boards from the decking of a wagon. The man sat on the coffin and waited.

Teen's father, face white, held the horns of his oxen to keep them from stampeding. "I can hear those guns yet", says aunt Teen.

Indians were met several times. The bucks always looked ready for battle, though seemingly friendly. Squaws carried their children tied to their backs with horsehair ropes. They wore blankets or buffalo robes and moccasins. Even 'friendly' Indians could not always be trusted. The tribes were realizing finally that the whites were taking the country away from them and they were desperate.

Aunt Teen came very near being trampled to death by her father's oxen in a sudden stampede one morning during a yoking up. Her neck was gashed by a hoof.

In a stampede on the prairie, her brother, 9 years old, was running trying to catch up. A following team and wagon would have run over him had not a man yanked out of the way.

Of course there were happier or more amusing times on the trip. For instance the fix Teen's mother got into. She was barefooted, and became marooned in a bed of cactus. Another woman carried her out.

And then there was the Great Cream Fight. Two Irish women were partners in a churn, but they had a quarrel and ended up with cream splashed all over themselves and all around.

A young woman was hurt fatally in a stampede of the oxen. Her baby was born dead. The children noticed the woman under a wagon and went to see what was going on. They were told the injured girl was sick. When they saw a woman holding the baby, they knew without being told that it was dead. Teen still is haunted by this memory.

An unknown man was found dead. There was nothing to show the cause of death, and he had his gun and also a fair sum of money.

One man left the train and went hunting alone, though warned of danger. An arrow almost struck him but he outwitted the lone Indian and shot him. Thereafter the hunter stuck close to the train.

Aunt Teen does not remember seeing any soldiers on the trail. A day came, August 9 when they needed help but there were no soldiers near. The Indians were well aware of it.

Near the American Falls of the Snake River, a train of 12 or 15 horse-drawn wagons, the 'New Yorkers', was ambushed. One man rode back a few miles to get help from Kennedy's train. A number of armed men hurried to the scene and later the ox train was brought up and encamped. Teen says it was the most awful sight, with dead people on the ground, dead and wounded horses, women and children crying, wagons burning; flour, sugar and feathers scattered on the earth where the Indians Had ripped sacks, beds and wagon covers to get cloth.

The Indians had driven off the horses. Kennedy got 25 men and tried to recapture some of the horses. The party was surrounded and fought for hours that hot day. They reached a few trees on a hill, but even so the situation was desperate and they might as well been killed had not another group of emigrants, the Missouri Train, come in sight about sundown. The Indians withdrew.

Seven men were killed and six were wounded, including the captain. The weapons then commonly used, even by soldiers were muzzleloaders. Breech-loading rifles were very scarce. A few Indians had guns, but most of them fought with bow and arrow and scalping knife.

Among those counted dead were two wounded men who had to be abandoned and could not be found later. Undoubtedly, Indians took them away. One had said all he wanted to do was stay and kill Indians.

Five dead men were carried in and laid down in the circle of wagons.

Among the wounded was Ephraim Taylor, shot through the side and back. The wound was cleansed by drawing a silk handkerchief through it, and he recovered.

A few wagons in poor condition were replaced by better ones that had belonged to the New Yorkers and the ox train went on. A woman wounded in the massacre died and was buried beside the trail August 12.

Word was received of two captive children in an Indian camp and several men went there and bought them, Teen says but she doesn't know what was traded for them, or what became of them. They were white, a boy and a girl, 4 or 6 years old. Seemingly they could not speak English, and were thin and ragged. The women cut off their tangled hair, which was full of lice and cleaned them up. Captain Kennedy took charge of them.

At camp on an alkali flat an Indian shot a guard. He was watched till daylight and killed when he tried to get away. Later twelve mounted Indians met the train and asked questions. They got no information but found the Indian. The emigrants feared trouble but nothing happened.

On through September the weary caravan went on. Lots of people wished they'd never come, Teen says. Every morning there were dead oxen with legs sticking up stiffly, poisoned by alkali.

Finally the emigrants looked down into the Grande Ronde Valley. It was beautiful, but the fall weather was chilly. "Don't you think after a country is settled it's not so cold?" asks Teen.

Emigrant trains usually began breaking up in the Grande Ronde. A few shacks could be seen and many stopped and took farms in 1862. John K. Kennedy settled there.

The Taylors and the two men traveling with them reached Walla Walla with one wagon dragged by one horse and one cow.

Walla Walla was the largest town in Washington Territory, but it was mostly shacks and ragged tents fluttering in the cold wind. It was October.

Christena Taylor married J. M. Chambers in 1873. They had seven children. There are three daughters still living. Mr. Chambers died in 1926, aged 80. "I've crossed the Cascades four times by covered wagon," declares Teen.

Alert, energetic, full of spunk, sensitive but tough, Aunt Teen has lived a long, toilsome, sometimes dangerous life, but it hasn't got her down, and her whimsical humor is irrepressible.

Thus the story ends of Christena Taylor Chambers, who crossed the plains at age 5, and now in 1950 is 92 years old.

Appendix 5

Sarah Zaring Howard: "The Covered Wagon and Personal Reminiscences", Written for the Garfield, Washington Women's Club about the year 1932 by Sarah Zaring Howard

On reading "The Covered Wagon", by Emerson Hough, many past memories of my childhood days are brought more vividly to my mind, of crossing the plains to our home in the West. Many places he mentions and happenings he records bring fresh to my mind the names of places I had forgotten and to my mind similar incidents to the ones recorded....

There were two thousand people in that great train headed by Captain Jesse Wingate, who reminds me in many ways of our own old captain; Molly Wingate (the captain's daughter) and her lover being the hero and heroine of the story.

My story has not that interesting feature of a hero and heroine, the young people of our train being like one big family of brothers and sisters. There were perhaps 300 people in our train and so far as I know, they were in the most part quite congenial to one another. Even at that I do not remember of any lovers and sweethearts.

Now to begin my story of crossing the plains: I think perhaps it was through the influence of our old captain himself who had been over the route to California in 1849 that my mother's people were inspired to start on so hazardous a journey and, my mother (who was a widow with two small children, my father having died two years previous) conceded to come with them.

Our preparations began weeks, or perhaps months before we started. It was sometime the very last of March 1862 that we bade farewell to our friends and relatives (who were to be left behind) and left our home in the southeastern part of the State of Iowa and wended our way to the western side of the state. When we reached the little town of Glenwood, a stop of several days was made. While there, my mother took her little girls to a picture gallery to get their pictures taken to leave with their grandparents. However, the pictures did not suit her and she did no leave them.

By the time our caravan all reached Omaha, several days, or perhaps weeks had elapsed, and it was now sometime near the middle of April. Omaha was then a small town and the bridge that spans the Missouri at that place did not exist. We crossed the river in a small ferry boat. I remember going with my aunt up into the little cabin of the boat where I could look out over the water.

After crossing the Missouri, we were then commencing our long and tedious journey and leaving all civilization and settlements behind. Our teams were the slow kind for the train was made up of cattle teams with exception of the captain's teams that were mules, which traveled ahead to spy out camping places where there were water and grass. The captain had pictured to his people a pleasurable trip with camping, fishing, hunting and traveling at leisure. However things were not always as they seem, and each day brought new trials. It seemed that we were somewhat like the children of Israel when they were wandering in the desert, and some felt like faltering by the way but they did not turn back.

One bright sunny day as we were moving along, we came in sight of our first Indians. They were of the Pawnee tribe and friendly to the whites. They were dressed in native garb, and armed with bows and arrows, and out for a hunt. Some of our men set up their whipstocks into the ground and placed pennies on them to see the Indians shoot them off.

It was not long now until we could see great camps or villages of Indians. I think there were hundreds of them in these camps. Their tents or camps were made of the skin of animals and set very close together. As long as we were among friendly tribes, these camps were visible, but when we came to the country where we did not find Indian camps, then we understood we were among hostile tribes.

Whenever we camped near the Indian village, the Indians would come in droves to our camp to beg or barter for some of the white man's foods. Sometimes they would bring fish to get something in exchange. Some of the women and girls of our camps would go to the Indian Camps to trade some little article for beads. I begged some of the folks to get some beads for me. At last my aunt said she would see what she could do about it, so she took a biscuit and went to the Indian camp and made a trade for beads. She came back with beads enough for both my sister and myself.

Very few animals of food value hovered near the road or our camps with the exception of some small game, and our people did not do much hunting for large game. However, I remember one time when we were in camp for several days some of the men went hunting. They had not been out very long until one man came to camp with the report that one of their number (a man who had a wife and two children in the camp) had accidentally killed himself by letting his revolver fall from his belt.

His little boy, five or six years old, on hearing that his father was dead, clapped his hands and said, "Oh, good! I'll have father's knife." I never forgot how that boy looked. I can see him yet.

As we traveled and neared the timber, the cattle began to run away at night. One night we were in country where the Indians showed hostilities and the cattle all stampeded or ran away; an old man who was a spiritualist got out of bed and climbed upon something where all could hear and shouted that the spirits had told him that all the people in the train were to be murdered before morning. You may be sure that there was not much sleep for anyone that night.

In a few days after that, just when we had come down from off a mountain into a valley, the cattle all stampeded while hitched to the wagons. They ran in all directions. Many people were more or less hurt, but only one woman was killed. The women and children being all in the wagons at the time and the place where the cattle ran was perfectly level, so the wagons did not upset. One of my uncle's wagons came uncoupled, the cattle running with the front wheels and leaving the hind wheels and the box by the roadside with my aunt and children in, but unhurt.

Hough tells in his book of their train regulations. Our train had similar rules of which he tells. Just when we were coming into the country where there was danger of Indians our captain had each wagon numbered and changed around each day so that all would share in the dangers alike, those traveling ahead or in the rear being in the greater danger.

Hough tells of crossing a river floating their wagons for boats. Well, our people crossed Green River in their wagon boxes (there being no ferry boat). Everything had to be unloaded from the wagons and the boxes made water tight. The wagons were taken to pieces and all loaded into the boxes and long ropes fastened to them so they could be pulled ashore. It was a very dangerous undertaking, however, and we did not have a very good feeling until all were safely on the opposite side of the river.

One day when we were traveling along at our usual gait and I think had rather become used to dangers we were in, we suddenly came in sight of eight wagons out a little way from the road. The wagons were stripped of everything and there were no teams in sight. When our train came nearer, two or three survivors of that train came to us and told their story – how the Indians had surprised them and came up while they were at their noon lunch. I think all the white people were killed but three, one man and two women. The Indians, being in a hurry to get away before our train came up, did not do quite as much, perhaps, as they would otherwise have done.

However, they carried off what they could and what they could not take they poured out in a heap and mixed everything in the way of food so that it could not be used, but left the wagons without burning them, which is their trait usually. Well, our people stopped and helped those people to find and bury their dead and gather up what they could find of the stock and a few articles of clothing which the Indians dropped in their hurry.

These people came in our train to the road turning off to California.

Somewhere near this time two of the young men of our train were missing while on guard with the stock. They were never found. Our captain was shot by the Indians about the same time. For days his life was despaired of and it was several weeks before he could be out again as we neared the end of our journey.

There were roads turning off to California and Southern Oregon, so our people were to say goodbyes to those going the different roads, for some went to California and some to Portland, Oregon, while my mother's people with a number of others came in by Boise City, Idaho, Boise being the first place to see a house since leaving Omaha, Nebraska. The forts Hough mentions in his book were still only tents with a few dugouts.

My story ends with crossing the mountains at La Grande, Oregon, and landing in the Walla Walla Valley, within a few miles of the then little town of Walla Walla, after having been five months on our way. We landed about September 15.

Appendix 6

Luellen Paul Garlington: "Recollections of a six months trek across the Plains and Mountains from Iowa to Oregon," 1976. Boulder, Colorado Genealogical Society 8 (2):23-27. Dictated earlier, and recorded by her daughter, Sue Garlington Cole.

I was born at Dahlonega, Iowa, November 24, 1852, and there my own father died when I was two years old. Three years later my mother, Ellen Paul married John McGuire, a widower, with four children. We then lived near Agency City, Wapello County, Iowa. John and Ellen Paul had three children, Lizzie (Maxson), Eva (Robley) and myself (Ellen). John McGuire, my half brother, about eight years younger than I, lives in Walla Walla now.

In the fall and winter of '61 many had the Western fever, and the McGuires and their neighbors made plans for the long trip to Oregon. They first sold their farm, then began the excitement of getting ready, purchasing oxen, wagons and supplies for the journey. Everything had to be in perfect condition for such an undertaking because we knew that when civilization was left behind we had to depend entirely on ourselves. What we did not have, we would have to do without.

Oxen were not plentiful, many had to use cows, working them with the oxen. The McGuires had two wagons with ox teams and one with a mule team. They had cows too, so they could change off and rest the oxen. Their wagon train was made up at Fremont, Iowa, and there were between forty and fifty wagons assembled. The captain of our train was John K. (called "J. K.") Kennedy, a brother-in-law of my stepfather. Other families in our train were the Scotts, Hoovers, Files, Zarings and the Kennedys. The Zarings were distant relatives of the McGuires.

There were two families of Pauls: Thomas, my father's brother, and their father, Joseph Paul, my grandfather. Their families were with them. Thomas Paul's wife died on the plains when her baby was born.

There were families traveling alone but when they reached the Indian country, they were always glad to join others for company and protection. We always camped over Sunday, while we rested and let the cattle rest, and always had church services, my grandfather Paul being the preacher. Leaving Fremont, we traversed thinly settled country, then the roads became poorer and the country rougher. Whenever we reached a house along the way we could be sure there would be a sign on the gate, "Eggs for Sale". Usually they were three or four cents a dozen. When they reached five cents no one thought we could afford them!

We saw Indians first in Nebraska. They were likely the Pawnees, who were "good" redskins, but just the same we children were afraid and were glad to keep hidden in the wagons. Our food was very plain. We could not take fresh vegetables as they were so perishable. Canned fruit and vegetables were then unknown. The fare was mostly meat and bread made of white flour mixed with salt and water and baked. Milk thickened with flour was a standby and of course it was nourishing and easily prepared. It was usually the evening meal.

Riding in heavy wagons on the rough trail was very tiresome. In the mornings the children used to like to walk ahead of the train, sometimes for hours at a time, until quite tired out. Then riding did not seem so bad. Roads were mostly deep ruts, at that time of year very dusty.

The first accident happened at Independence Rock, so named of a great rock near a large river, one of the regular camping places along the trail. We camped there while the men hunted. One of them, George Bovee, returned and said he had killed a wolf. The others joked him and refused to believe him, so he said he would bring in the pelt, but in stooping over, his revolver dropped and struck a rock, killing him. He was buried there.

After reaching the plains, hundreds of miles from any settlement, it got so hot and dry the cattle could hardly travel for want of water. Then they began to get so wild the slightest noise made them stampede. A Mrs. Townsend jumped from a wagon one day during a stampede and was run over and killed. All who died on the trail were buried at the place of death.

Each night wagons were drawn in a circle so a corral was thus made with livestock inside of it, to prevent a stampede, which of course would be more terrible at night than during daylight. One morning as oxen were being yoked up a dog barked and instantly a stampede started, cattle starting wildly in all directions. It was in a mountainous section and we knew Indians were bad thereabouts. All the younger men set out on foot to hunt for the cattle. It seemed an almost hopeless task. The older men remained with the women and children.

One day a man came riding like mad on his tired horse, back to our train for help, from a train a few miles ahead of ours, a wealthy outfit with a dozen or more wagons, all horse-drawn and well provisioned, from New York and were crossing the plains only for adventure and excitement. During the day they drove alone but at night they always tried to join another train. Redskins had attacked them and this man had ridden back to us for help. Captain Kennedy hurried a number of men ahead, but when they arrived the Indians had gone, after killing five of the party, taking all the horses, cattle and provisions – even their feather beds and wagon covers.

That night the men hunted and attacked the Indians but did not recover anything. One of the men was killed, his body was hidden in the sage brush when he fell, but his body was not found. Whenever bodies of those killed were found they were buried by the roadside and these graves marked by signs reading, "Killed by Indians", as warning to other travelers. During this attack when everything was in confusion and everyone trying to escape, a Miss Adams, who had got almost out of reach of the redskins, looked back and saw her poor old mother trying to follow her. She ran back to help, but was shot and died a couple of hours later. Her brother was killed in an effort to rescue their horses and cattle.

In our train was a Dr. Collins, who had no family but who had a driver and a fine team for his wagon. He was most capable and took care of the sick and injured. All who could spare them gave cattle to the New Yorkers but even then there were not enough for their wagons, so their families were divided up to ride in our train. It was said their train had been watched for some days by the reds because they surmised it was a wealthy outfit. Also it was strongly believed the Mormons were helping the redskins, for during the attack our men were sure they heard voices of whites giving orders to the Indians and were convinced they were the voices of Mormons.

Some of the reds had guns and others used poisoned arrows. One of our men had a spyglass, which was our greatest treasure in Indian country. On the plains the reds could be detected at a great distance, long before we could be seen by them.

While traveling along the Snake River we could see an old Indian watching and following us for days. Of course we couldn't tell whether he was spying for a band of reds or maybe just watching for a chance to steal some of our horses. One night we camped on the river bank where water was low. Nearby the river branched and the land was wild and rough, likely known as "the bad lands." Great boulders and cliffs made it an ideal hiding spot for Indians.

That night the old redskin crept in among the rocks and shadows and killed one of our guards with a poisoned arrow. There were four guards each night so the other three gave chase but the rocks prevented their catching him. Next morning, several of our men soon tracked him down, shot and left him where he fell. For days after, we were fearful his companions would attack us, but apparently he'd been alone and they'd not yet learned of his death.

Horses and cattle were getting very tired, going for long hours without water and often without feed. Grass, when there was any, was scorched dry. One day a cow became so tired and thirsty she couldn't travel any longer in the heat of the day so was left to be brought on in the cool of the evening. But the reds found her and cut away part of a hind quarter and left her. Our men killed her and hurried back to camp for they knew the reds were lurking nearby.

The beautiful Green River was clear and deep and wide. On seeing it our first thought was how we could ever get across. It was decided to make boats of the wagons, which were taken apart, rags and rosin were used to caulk them so they would be water tight. This was such a slow and awkward means of crossing it required three days to complete and get wagons ready to travel again.

It was a comical sight, the men trying to paddle these queer looking crafts, and it provided much amusement for the youngsters after strenuous days of travel. Hardest task was to get the cattle started over. We drove them to the bank and every man, woman and child waved branches and pushed and shouted till finally the foremost horses and cows started into the water. After that it was easy for the others followed, and it was a beautiful sight to see them swimming across the wide river.

In September of '62 we reached the Grande Ronde Valley and Eastern Oregon. How happy we all were as we approached the valley and realized the long, hard days on the trail were over and that we need not fear the Indians any more and could lie down at night and sleep untroubled. We found scattered settlers and it was a delight to meet and talk with them. This was a beautiful valley in a beautiful time of year.

The settlement was likely Union Town. Here the train split up, some going on to California, some to other parts of Oregon and some, including the McGuires, went on to Walla Walla, then but a few houses and a school. This group included about twenty families. The main reason the McGuires did not remain in the Grande Ronde Valley where they'd planned to settle was that the wind blew so hard while we were camped there that the wagons had to be staked down so they would not blow over! Our destination was a camp on Cottonwood Creek, about five miles from Walla Walla.

In spite of all the hardships we children did enjoy most of the long trek. Camping out, cooking over campfires, new scenes every day – these were all a joy to us. My step-sister, Lizzie McGuire, was one of the most mischievous of the children. I remember one evening we camped near a small creek over which former campers had laid a huge log. Lizzie slipped back to camp from our play and brought a bar of soap and soaped the log good. Then we all hid to watch the fun when any of the grownups tried to cross on the log.

Appendix 7

Margaret Stoot Thiel: "Pioneer Relates Exciting Trip across the Plains", An interview published in a Walla Walla newspaper in 1926, furnished by Jayne Allison McCarley, great, great-granddaughter of John K. Kennedy

I was born in Iowa on March 19, 1846, so I have passed my 80th milestone. My father John Stoot was born in Kentucky. My mother's maiden name was Sarah McGuire. She also was born in Kentucky. My father died when I was two years old and mother married John Kennedy of Indiana, a widower who had two daughters and one son. Mother had three daughters and one son. My stepfather, John Kennedy had gone to California shortly after gold was discovered there and had later returned to his home in Iowa. Still later he made another trip across the plains, staying a year or two. When I was 16 years old he decided to go west once more, to stay this time.

The Civil War had broken out and a good many people, who didn't want to get mixed up in it were heading for Montana, Oregon or California. I didn't want to leave Iowa, for my sweetheart had enlisted in an Iowa regiment and I was afraid if we made the long trip across the plains to Oregon, something would happen and we would never get married. I was only 16 and had no folks to stay with, so when my stepfather and mother and the rest of the family got ready for the trip across the plains, in the spring of 1862, about the only thing I could do was to go along. With soldiers moving around as they did during the Civil War, and with letters getting lost, my lover didn't get my letter, and of course, when we left we didn't know where we were going to settle, so he didn't know where to write to me.

When we got to the Grande Ronde Valley it was late in the season, so we decided to winter there. The result was that my father took up 160 acres near La Grande and that became our home. I got a job cooking and waiting on the table at the hotel in La Grande. Wash Ewing, the proprietor, wanted to marry me. I hadn't heard from my lover, and as the war was at its height and thousands of soldiers were being killed, my folks thought he might be dead and that I would be foolish not to marry Mr. Ewing, so on June 9, 1864, I was married to Mr. Ewing. My Iowa sweetheart came back from the war safe and finally located me, but I was married. We never saw each other again, but I heard from friends of mine back there that he got married a few years after the war. He died many years ago.

My stepfather, John Kennedy sold our place in Mahaska County, Iowa and turned all of our property into money. Nine other families near us wanted to come west, so they promised that if my stepfather would buy wagons and oxen for them to cross the plains, they would return the money he spent, with good interest, when they got to Oregon. He outfitted these nine families. When they got out there, they promised him that if they ever got any money ahead that they could spare, they would pay him what they owed, but he never got a cent from them.

My two brothers, my four sisters, two of whom were married, with myself and my mother and stepfather, started from Iowa on May 5. We had a good outfit and my stepfather put in enough provisions to last four months, for he figured that we could make the trip in that length of time. There were nearly 100 wagons in the wagon train. They elected by stepfather Captain, as he already had made two trips across the plains.

On the Platte River we met a large party of Indians. I think they were Pawnees, though I am not sure. Alvin Zehring, who was a member of our wagon train and who is now a resident of Walla Walla, said to a huge Indian who had a dog with him: "You savvy swap?" The young Indian nodded. Alvin pointed to me and said, "I'll swap you this girl for your dog." The Indian picked up his dog, thrust it into Alvin's arms, turned to where I stood, grabbed me up and started away. Alvin, hearing my screams, hollered to the Indian, "I was just joking." The Indian paid no attention, and kept on going.

I was frightened nearly to death. I scratched the Indians face. He grabbed my arms and held them to my sides. I reached around, and caught his hair and jerked his head back. I kicked and struggled but I was helpless. Meanwhile my stepfather called to the Indian, "Drop her – Drop her." But the Indian had swapped in good faith and refused to go back on the deal. By this time a dozen men with guns had started after us. I heard my stepfather say to them, "Don't shoot, don't shoot the Indian, you'll kill my girl. Shoot over them." A moment later a volley of bullets whistled over our heads. The Indian dropped me and stalked away. For two or three weeks after that I used to wake up at night screaming, thinking the Indian had me.

Before leaving Iowa, my stepfather had bought four riding horses and four side-saddles for myself and my sisters. We would ride ahead of the train, select a camping place and gather wood or buffalo chips and by the time the wagon train had caught up with us, we had the camp fires going. Our horses died on the plains and as the cattle were getting gaunt and weak my stepfather wouldn't let us put the side saddles in the wagon. I carried my side saddle two days before I finally abandoned it by the side of the road.

I think it was at Green River, though I am not sure whether that was the name of the river or not, that we had to pay $1.50 for each wagon to be ferried over. Some Mormons were running the ferry. We learned after that there was a good ford about a mile and a half below the ferry. It took a long time for our train to be ferried across the river, for there were several hundred other wagons that we called the "Honey Moon Special". Most of them were young folks, newlyweds. Instead of oxen they were using horses for their wagons. They had the finest outfits.

The Mormons at the ferry had provisions for sale. They had a number of large cheeses. One of the young men, a member of the Honey Moon Special party, asked the price of one of the big cheeses. Some of the others had urged him not to buy it, as the price was so high, but he said, "Don't worry, I'm the fellow that has the money. I can buy the cheese all right, and taking out a long buckskin purse, he untied the string and purse [and set] a handful of gold pieces on the board which served as a counter. He pocketed his change and bore the cheese triumphantly away. A number of Mormons and Indians were standing around at the time he displayed his money. The next day their party was attacked by Indians and he and a number of others were killed, their livestock was run off and they were left stranded.

Next day the members of the "Honeymoon Special" preceded us on their way westward. That afternoon, a member of their party arrived at our wagon train with his horse covered with sweat and lather, and said, "The Indians are attacking our wagon train." My stepfather halted our wagon train and asked for volunteers to go ahead and help the train being attacked. A number of the men, particularly the single men, volunteered and hurried forward to drive off the Indians. When they reached the vicinity of the other train, they found the Indians greatly outnumbered the rescuing party. They attacked the rescuing party. They shot my step-father in the side. They tied my stepfather on a horse and rode back to our wagon train as fast as they could to protect their own families.

When we reached the other wagon train, we found the Indians and the white men dressed up to look like Indians had taken all of the horses and had killed a number of men in the other party. One member of our party who had gone to rescue was killed. He left a wife and five children. The Indians took his body with them and we never recovered it. Among the men who were killed in the "Honeymoon Special" were two young men who were coming to Oregon with their sisters. Those who had not been killed in the wagon train ahead of us were taken into our train. I will never forget the grief of these two sisters when the men brought in the bodies of their brothers, both of whom had been scalped. We buried the dead by the side of the road.

When the party had been attacked, the men had stacked the feather beds inside the wagons and made the women lie down in the wagons while the men tried to fight the Indians. The Indians however rode past the back of the wagons and shot at the women from the rear of the wagon. One of the young women climbed out of the wagon and, holding a heavy bread board in front of her, tried to escape, but an Indian shot through the bread board, the bullet penetrating her jugular vein. She fell and bled to death within a few moments. The Indians ripped open the feather beds, throwing the feathers out on the prairie and taking the ticks. They also ripped open the sacks of flour, shook out the flour and took the flour sacks.

When our wagon train came to where the other train had been attacked, we tried to gather up some of the flour, and also to gather up the feathers. In scooping up the feathers, one of the party came across a purse with over $800 in it. The owner had hidden the purse in the feather bed.

My stepfather as captain of the train, told the members of the train that had been attacked that they could travel with us, so we took the best of their wagons, their bacon and what flour we could gather up and other supplies and started out. We took in our wagons the two girls whose brothers had been killed and scalped. They traveled with us as far as Fort Boise.

My stepfather's wound in the side bothered him, so we had to lay over for two or three weeks till it healed. That's why we were so late getting to the Grande Ronde Valley. The whole wagon train decided to wait, so as to rest the stock. A week or two after we started on, we were overtaken by another wagon train who were using horses instead of oxen. That night an Indian tried to stampede their horses. He shot one of the guards in the arm. This was just before daylight. The men in our train and in the other train started out after the Indian with dogs. The dogs tracked him to where he was hidden. He started running [and] the men began shooting at him. He had great vitality for he kept running after he had been shot four times. Finally one of the men in our train caught up with him and, as his gun was unloaded, hit him over the head with it, killing the Indian and wrecking the gun.

One thing we dreaded almost more than Indians and that was stampedes. Sometimes the oxen would stampede because they were frightened by a storm at night, or when we were traveling cross the fresh trail of buffalo and that would sometimes make them stampede. The men tried to remedy the situation by putting rings in the noses of the oxen and having the driver hold onto the end of the rope. But this was [not a success], for once started, nothing seemed to stop the frightened animals.

One day a Mrs. Townsend was standing on the board wagon tongue when one of these stampedes occurred. Her 18 month old son was riding in the covered wagon, but when the oxen broke, she shouted to a hired man, "What shall I do, jump or get back in the wagon?" "Jump" the man shouted. She jumped, but didn't fall clear of the wagon. The heavy wheels passed over her, and when we picked her up, she was so badly crushed that she only lived a few minutes. Had she climbed back into the wagon she wouldn't have been hurt, for the stampede was stopped before the wagons were overturned or much damage had been done, her little baby escaping without harm.

Instead of being four months on the road, we were six months. There were nine in our family besides the hired man. Traveling on foot and being out in the open all the time gives you a big appetite, so the first thing we knew, we were out of coffee, sugar, bacon, tea, and flour. Father paid $20 for a sack of flour and mother bought a pint of syrup for a dollar.

After crossing the Blue Mountains, we camped on the edge of the Grande Ronde Valley, where we pitched camp, for we had only four yoke of oxen left and we were out of provisions. Father went to Walla Walla to buy supplies. A few days after he left, a horse-drawn outfit camped with us. I don't know whether they were miners or freighters, but I do know that they had all sorts of provisions, which they insisted on sharing with us. They camped with us for two or three days. Mother went through their wagons and got all of their dirty clothes, which we girls washed. One of the men said their mules needed a rest, so they would stay over a few days, but I think it was mother's cooking or the sake of visiting us girls that they really stayed over. It was three weeks before father got back from Walla Walla with provisions.

My stepfather, John Kennedy took up a place near La Grande in the fall of 1862...On June 9, 1864, I married Wash Ewing, proprietor of the hotel where I was working at La Grande. My sister Cassie married the year before I was.

I will never forget the first time I saw my brother-in-law, John L. Caviness. As he rode up to our place, my sister Cassie and I looked out and saw he was a stranger. He was a fine looking man. He was well dressed and had a good horse. My sister said to me, "You leave him alone, he's mine, I saw him first. I said "Who is he?" She said, "It don't matter who he is, he is going to be my husband". When he came in he told us he had a message from our half-brother, Robert Kennedy. He had been working in the mines with him. Rob had come west in 1857. Mr. Caviness stayed two or three weeks at our home. They have celebrated their 60th wedding anniversary, so you see my sister not only got him, but she succeeded in keeping him...

My sisters, Susan Jane and Mary Kennedy had a double wedding. Jane Married Tim Neely and Mary married a man named Alfred Allison. My stepfather, John Kennedy was sheriff at that time. My husband, Wash Ewing, sold the hotel after we had been married about a year, and we took up a place on Dry Creek, three miles from Walla Walla. We sold that place and bought 16 acres on the edge of Walla Walla. Mr. Ewing and I had four children, all of whom are dead.

After Mr. Ewing's death, I married a Dry Creek farmer named F. W. Theil. He was born in Prussia. He was thrifty and a hard worker. We had two children, both boys. Walter lives at Stockton and Fred here at Oxnard. My sister Mrs. Neely, who lives at Vancouver, Wash. and myself are the only ones of the family now living. I married Mr. Thiel 42 years ago. We had pretty hard sledding at first, for wheat was only 50 cent a bushel and times were pretty hard. One time a neighbor asked my husband how he was getting along and I heard him say, "Everything I've got is mortgaged except the old woman and the chickens, and I'll be doggoned if I am going to mortgage them." That year we raised an unusually large wheat crop. It ran over 40 bushels to the acre. All the neighbors advised us to hold our wheat, as it was going to bring a big price. We sold at .95 a bushel and the neighbors who advised us to hold our wheat sold at around 60 or 70 cents a bushel. That one crop got us out of debt.

Appendix 8

Medorem Crawford, Capt. A. Q. M., Commanding Emigrant Escort, "Notice Posted to Emigrants"

The undersigned having been for two years past connected with Government Escorts for the protection of emigrants on the road to Oregon and Washington Territory and being detailed by the Secretary of War for similar service this season, would take this method to advise persons intending to emigrate, as to outfit, time of starting, etc., etc.

None but the good, new medium-sized wagons, with iron axletree or thimble skein, should be used. Wagons should not be loaded more than half their capacity. Mules or oxen should be used. Horses will not do to depend upon for service. The cheapest and best teams is medium-sized active young oxen. No kind of stock will pay to take over on speculation and emigrants should avoid taxing themselves with too much labor. An ordinary two head wagon with eighteen hundred weight, good double cover and three yoke of light active cattle, are the best outfit a man can have. A few extra animals in each company, would be an excellent precaution against accidents and extra shoes and nails should be provided for horses and mules. Plenty of wagon grease should be provided and freely used.

The time required from the Missouri River, to the Settlements, will not vary much from one hundred days, with teams. Each person should take at least 250 pounds of provisions; one half of which should be flour, 50 pounds of bacon and the balance in sugar, coffee, tea, rice, dried fruit, etc. etc. There should be at least two men to each wagons, as the labor of driving and taking care of a team and wagon, is more than one man can perform, in addition to other camp labor. Each man should be well armed and keep his gun convenient and ready for use on the shortest notice. No furniture or extra baggage of any kind should be carried; nothing but what is actually required on the journey.

Before leaving the Settlements, companies should be organized in parties of not less than thirty and no more than sixty wagons. One of your number should be chosen Captain and one for Train Master. Your officers should then make a vigilant examination and inspection of every man's wagon, teams, arms, ammunition, provisions etc., and no man should be allowed to join a company unless properly outfitted, otherwise you will have persons in your company unable to keep up, or otherwise deficient, which deficiency will have to be supplied by the company, or the persons left destitute on the plains. Your Captain should decide and order when to start, when and where to camp and his orders should be implicitly obeyed. He should also decide all questions or disputes arising in your company and his decision should be final whether right or wrong.

Your Train Master should travel always with the train and see that those in the lead do not travel too fast or those in the rear fall too far behind. He should look for the best crossings of streams and bad places in the road and give directions for doubling teams at bad hills. By having one thus to direct, if he is promptly obeyed, much time will be saved.

At the end of a day's travel, the Captain, having selected the camp, the Train Master should direct where the animals are to be watered and where the best grass is to be found. Each driver should see that his team has plenty of water and drive then to grass as soon as possible after arriving in camp. The Captain and Train Master should be relieved, at the expense of the company, from giving any special attention to their own teams, while on the march and from guard duty.

For guard duty, the men of your company should be equally divided into three divisions or squads, one of which is constantly on duty, under the direction of an officer, selected by the Captain, who for convenience may be call Sergeant. These squads should be equally divided and these sub-divisions relieve each other during the twenty-four hours they are on duty. The herd should never be left, day or night, without guards and a guard should also be kept in camp at nights. The firing of guns in camp should be strictly prohibited and the report of a gun or pistol after dark should be a signal for all hands to rally with arms.

Take no dogs along, for they are a continual source of annoyance, and seldom live to get over the barren country along the Snake River.

The escort under my charge will consist of about fifty armed men. I shall leave Omaha about the 20th of May or as soon after as possible. My route will be up the Platte River, thence up the Sweetwater, over the Lander Road, leaving that road and crossing the Snake River a short distance this side of old Fort Hall. There will doubtless be a ferry established for the convenience of emigrants, in that vicinity. With the road on the north side of Snake River, I am not personally acquainted but am well satisfied that it is much better than the old route, on the south side, my information being based upon representations of emigrants who traveled that road last season.

This road will lead emigrants directly to the Boise mines, which will be found about 300 miles from the crossing of Snake River. This road will be preferable as well to those desiring to go to settled portions of Oregon and Washington Territory, as to those going to the mines, as there is a well traveled road from these mines to Walla Walla.

As friendly Indians often visit Emigrant camps for trade, care should be taken not to encourage too much familiarity. They should not be allowed inside the camp. If you have business with them, transact it outside.

After leaving the Platte River, no person should leave the camp alone, and it is dangerous for small parties to be far from the camp or train.

Be sure to drive slow in the start. Your teams should pass the first Eight Hundred Miles without losing either flesh or spirits. This escort is intended to protect emigrants as far as possible against Indian depredations, but unless emigrants will use the necessary precautions to insure their safety, they are liable to suffer in spite of any assistance I shall be able to render them.

By organizing, in this manner and observing these simple rules, you will avoid most, if not all the difficulties and losses to which emigrants are usually subjected.

Medorem Crawford, Capt. A. Q. M.,

Commanding Emigrant Escort

Appendix 9

Final entry in the journal of Robert C. Scott

"September 29...We are now in Walla Walla, Wash. [Finding] no work at Auburn, Oregon, we packed our horses and started out and kept going, looking for a place to winter and work, and landed here, 300 miles from Auburn. We are out of money and have to do something. Personally I do not have a dollar. I walked down the street here and a man asked me if I wanted a job. My reply was quickly yes. He asked me if I could drive an ox team. I looked at him and smiled, saying I have just landed here from Iowa, driving ox train through and 5 months on the way. (I am so tired driving oxen I never wanted to see another ox train.)

The man said to take this ox whip and this 5 yoke team and loaded wagon to Lewiston and bring back a load. The trip took 5 days. I took the whip and jumped on the wagon, after sending word to my mess friends where I was going and to wait here for my return. When I returned they had a cabin to stay in. Was paid $5 a day and expenses, so I did eat and bought some grub for the bunch. So we were fixed for a start in Walla Walla, our destination when we left Fremont, Iowa April 24th. We found work in Walla Walla, enough to live on, but were not satisfied with that and began to think about something else better. We wanted to do mining, that's what we came here to do, and for ourselves if possible. January 12, 1863"

Bibliography

Chambers, Christena Taylor, "Covered wagons real to her, trail life rugged, aged woman recalls"; Sunday Portland Oregonian Magazine, February 9, 1950; Article written by Phillip P. Olson.

Crawford, Medorem, Capt. A. W. M., Commanding Emigrant Escort. "Notice Posted to emigrants"; included as Appendix 16 of "The Diary of J. S. McClung, Oregon Trail, 1862", Lewis and Clark College, November 1977.

Crawford, Medorem, Capt. A. W. M., "The report and journal of Captain Medorem Crawford, 1862"; in Senate Executive Document 17, 37th Congress, 3rd Series, January 8, 1863, p 12.

Cummins, Robert, "Reminiscences"; dated July 2, 1901, in Zola Burnap Irwin's "Westward Ho with the Cummins Family"; Jonas Babcock Chapter, DAR, Nat. No. 646, Spokane, Wash.

Cummins, Woodson, Conversations with the author.

DeVoto, Bernard, "The Year of Decision: 1846", Boston, 1943

Fitzsimmons, Martha McGuire, "Pioneer Daughters thrilled by talks"; East Washingtonian, Pomeroy, Wash., November 12, 1942.

Garlington, Luellen Paul, "Recollections of a six months trek across the plains and mountains from Iowa to Oregon, 1976", Colorado Genealogical Society 8 (2): 23-27. Dictated earlier and recorded by her daughter, Sue Cole.

Gould, Jane Holbrook, "Jane A. Gould: Her Journal", Copied from a Typewritten carbon copy, loaned by T. T. Tourtillott, son of Jane Gould; By Phillip O. Olson, Oswego, Oregon, 1951; includes some explanatory notes by Mr. Tourtillott.

Hewitt, R. H. "Notes by the Way, Memoranda of a Journey across the Plains", Olympia; Printed at the Washington Standard, 1863; Reprint Frank McCaffrey, Publishers, Seattle, 1955, July 25, 1862; journal entry, 28.

Hillman, John C., "Letter to Mrs. Bronson", dated August 11, 1862; Incorporated in Hamilton Scott's "Wagon Train West, 1862", August 9 entry.

Howard, Sarah Zaring, "The Covered wagon and personal reminiscences", from a typescript in the possession of the author. Note at end reads, "Written for the Garfield Women's Club about the year 1932, by Sarah Zaring Howard. Garfield is in Whitman County, Washington.

Judson, Henry M., "Diary of Henry M. Judson, Omaha to Oregon, 1862", Nebraska State Historical Society, No. 358, MS 953; excerpts of August 9, 1862 entry incorporated in "Oregon Trail Emigrant Massacre of 1862, Bert Webber, Webb Research Group, 1987.

Langum, David J., "Pioneer Justice on the Overland Trails", The Western Historical Quarterly, Vol. V, number 4, October 1974, by Utah State University, Logan, Utah, 421-439.

Mattes, Merrill J., "The Platte River Road Narratives", Urbana: University of Illinois Press, 1988.

McCarley, Ella Jane Allison, "John Knox Kennedy, Pioneer of Washington State", Clark County, Washington Genealogical Society Library.

Maxson, Mary Elizabeth Paul, "Wagon Train Emigrant here since 1862 has Anniversary"; Union-Bulletin, Walla Walla, Wash., October 4, 1941.

McClung, James Scott, "The Diary of J. S. McClung; Oregon Trail, 1862" The James S. McClung papers, MSS 1508, Oregon Historical Society, Portland.

Packard, Pat and Marjorie Ellis Miles, "Reconstruction of Roster of 1862 Kennedy Company, John K. Kennedy Captain", Idaho Genealogical Society Quarterly 36, (April 1993): 54.

Palmer, Joel, "Journal of Travels over the Rocky Mountains to the Mouth of the Columbia River...", Cincinnati, J. A. and U. P. James, 1847.

Reid, John Phillip, "Policing the Elephant, Crime, Punishment and Social Behavior on the Overland Trail, 1997", Huntington Library, San Marino, California.

San Francisco Evening Bulletin, September, 27, 1862 news story about the Indian attack of August, 9, 1862, incorporated in "Oregon Trail Emigrant Massacre, 1862"; Bert Webber, Webb Research Group, 1987.

Scott, Hamilton, "A trip across the plains in 1862", in Idaho State Historical Society Library, Boise.

Scott, Robert, "Robert Scott's trip to Washington with oxen in 1862"; Manuscript Archives Collections of the Idaho Historical Society.

Swazley, H. F., Letter published in the Union, a newspaper of Quincy, Ill. October 28, 1862, describing the August 9, 1862 Indian attack, incorporated in "Oregon Trail Emigrant Massacre, 1862", Bert Webber, Webb Research Group, 1987.

Thiel, Margaret Stoot, "Pioneer relates exciting trip across the plains", an Interview published in a Walla Walla newspaper in 1926; furnished by Jayne Allison McCarley, great-great granddaughter of John K. Kennedy.

Unruh, John D. Jr., "The Plains Across", University of Illinois Press, Urbana and Chicago,1979.

Webber, Bert, "Oregon Trail Emigrant Massacre, 1862", Webb Research Group, 1987.

About the Author

The author was born on the Eastern Washington farm his ancestors established in 1862. It was in 1862 that his great-grandfather, Robert Cummins crossed the plains and mountains from Iowa to Washington Territory with the John Knox Kennedy wagon train.

The author remembers his grandfather, Woodson Cummins entertaining his grandchildren with stories about a firing squad execution and about hostile Indians, events his grandfather remembered from his experience crossing the continent with the Kennedy train, as a seven year old boy.

Wanting to find the truth behind his grandfather's tales, Everell Cummins collected a variety of source information about the Kennedy train, from diaries and old news stories. A number of other Kennedy train descendants, also interested in learning more about the Kennedy train, helped in that effort. Now Cummins has written a day by day account of what developed as a particularly eventful wagon train crossing. Did the information he found verify his grandfather's stories? Some did and some did not.

Articles about the Kennedy train written by Everell Cummins have appeared in Columbia Magazine, a publication of the Washington State Historical

Society and in the Overland Journal, the magazine of the Oregon-California Trails Association.

The author and his wife Marie now live in San Rafael, California.

Made in the USA
Monee, IL
07 May 2023

33264851R00144